The Amazing Space Almanac

Justin Segal

illustrations by
Carol Lyon

A Roxbury Park Book

LOWELL HOUSE JUVENILE

LOS ANGELES

NTC/Contemporary Publishing Group

Published by Lowell House
A division of NTC/Contemporary Publishing Group, Inc.
4255 West Touhy Avenue, Lincolnwood (Chicago), Illinois 60646-1975 U.S.A.
© 1998 by Lowell House

Lowell House books can be purchased at special discounts when ordered in bulk for premiums and special sales. Contact Department CS at the following address:
NTC/Contemporary Publishing Group
4255 West Touhy Avenue
Lincolnwood, IL 60646-1975
1-800-323-4900

Library of Congress Cataloging-in-Publication Data

Segal, Justin
    The Amazing Space Almanac/ by Justin Segal
       p.   cm.
    Summary: Discusses the many aspects of space, including the origin and nature of the universe, the history of space travel, quarks, quasars, black holes, and extraterrestrials.
      ISBN 1-56565-691-1
      1.   Astronomy—Juvenile literature. 2. Astronomy—Miscellaneous—Juvenile literature.
          [1. Astronomy. 2. Astronomy—Miscellanea.]
  I.   Title.
  QB46.S35 1998
  520—DC21

                                  98-21958
                                     CIP
                                     AC

Roxbury Park is a division of NTC/Contemporary Publishing Group, Inc.

Managing Director and Publisher: Jack Artenstein
Editor in Chief, Roxbury Park Books: Michael Artenstein
Director of Publishing Services: Rena Copperman
Managing Editor: Lindsey Hay
Designer: Justin Segal

Printed and bound in the United States of America
10 9 8 7 6 5 4 3 2 1

dedicated to Carl Sagan, who showed me the way up

• ACKNOWLEDGMENTS •

Special thanks go to astronaut Dr. David Wolf, whose "letters from space" provided a unique view on life in orbit; Eileen Hawley from NASA's Office of Public Affairs (Johnson Space Center), whose kind permission allowed material to be included in this book; Alice S. Wessen from the Public Affairs Office of the Jet Propulsion Laboratory (JPL), for keeping me "in the loop"; and, most of all, to the vision and patience of my editor at Lowell House, Lindsey Hay. Without their efforts, this mission would have failed.

Contents

Foreword
Author's Note 7

The Whole Wide Universe
Making Space 8
Twelve Universal Laws 12
Our Ten-Dimensional Universe 15
Galaxies 16
Superclusters 17
Stars 17

Our Solar System
The Sun 21
The Planets 23
Mysterious Planets 37
Many, Many Moons 38
More Moon Mysteries 41

Cosmic Mysteries
Is the Universe Infinite? 42
The Mystery of the Missing Neutrinos 42
The Mystery of Dark Matter 43
A Mysterious Attraction 43
The Mystery of Antimatter 44
The Mystery of Gravitons 44
The Mystery of Time 44
Black Holes 45
Does Extraterrestrial Life Exist? 47

The Space Age Begins

First Steps 50
The Space Race 53
The Dangers of Space Travel 59
Space Disasters 60
The Astronauts' Memorial 66

Unmanned Space Probes

Back to the Moon at Last 67
A Return to the Red Planet 69
The *Galileo* Mission 71
The Last of the Giant Spaceships 74
Pioneer 10 Says Good-bye 77
Voyager Says Hello 78
A Probe to the Sun 79
Flying Into the Future 80

Exploring Space from Earth

Space Calendars Made of Stone 81
Eyes in the Sky 83
Better Ways to See the Stars 87
Asteroid Impacts 89

Life in Space

What It Takes to Become an Astronaut 93
Training for Weightlessness 94
Launch Preparations 96
Living in Space 98

Space Stations

A Station Called *Skylab* 102
A Station Called "Peace" 103
A Space Place Without a Name 104
An Emergency Trip Home 105

Space and the Future

The Space Plane 107
The Next Generation of Flying Observatory 107
Capturing Comets 108
A Trip to the Beginning of Time 108
The *Pluto Express* 109
Collecting the Solar Wind 109
Guiding by the Stars 110
A Fleet of Tiny Spaceships 110
Space Colonies 111
Beam Me Up, NASA 113
The Death of Our Sun 113
The Big Crunch 114

Further Exploration

Kids in Space 115
Space Web sites 118
Space Books 120
Space Films and Videos 122
Space CD-ROMs 123

Appendix

An Astronaut's Journal 125

Index

. . . . 127

FOREWORD

• AUTHOR'S NOTE •

When I was ten years old, I wanted to be an astronaut. I read every book I could find about space, bought a telescope of my own, and spent long hours gazing at the night sky.

I even wrote to NASA for an application to become an astronaut. Back then, though (this was in the years before the Space Shuttle), it seemed as if most astronauts spent their whole careers waiting for a mission instead of flying in space. Today the story is different: Spaceflights are launched all the time, and no matter the time of year, astronauts are always in Earth's orbit. It's a very exciting time for space travelers.

This book is dedicated to every child who ever looked up to the stars and planets, wondered what they look like up close, and wished he or she could visit.

— Justin Segal

THE WHOLE WIDE UNIVERSE

Our universe is the greatest mystery known to man. Where did everything come from? How was life created? Will it ever end? These are riddles whose answers lie in the stars. Today our window on the universe is clearer than ever before. Telescopes, space probes, and astronauts have brought the heavens closer to Earth. Many of our questions have begun to be answered.

• MAKING SPACE •

Throughout history, there have been many different beliefs about the origin of the universe. Here are a few of them:

The Big Bang. Astronomers believe the universe was created in an instantaneous explosion from a single point in space. This "Big Bang," some fifteen billion years ago, is the reason our universe is still expanding today.

◀ WAS THE UNIVERSE CREATED IN A "BIG BANG"?

TIMELINE OF THE UNIVERSE

THE UNIVERSE IS BORN IN A BIG BANG FROM AN INFINITELY SMALL, DENSE POINT

GRAVITY AND PHYSICS (MATTER & ENERGY) ARE BORN

THE UNIVERSE HAS EXPANDED. ELEMENTARY PARTICLES ARE BORN

PROTONS AND NEUTRONS ARE BORN

15 BILLION YEARS AGO 10^{-43} SECONDS 10^{-34} SECONDS 10^{-6} SECONDS

A wrestling match among the gods. The ancient Sumerian people, living 6,000 years ago along the Mediterranean Sea, believed our world was the result of a mud-wrestling match among the gods. The Earth was formed from a dirt clod thrown into the air.

Fire sends sparks into the nighttime sky. African bushmen believe that the sparks from a burning fire, floating upward into the nighttime sky, became shining stars and formed the universe.

The Chief of the Sky Spirits visits our world. The Modoc Indians of North America believe the Chief of the Sky Spirits tired of the Above World (space) and decided to visit the Earth. Where his feet touched the ground, he created trees. Snow melted under his feet and became rivers. Pieces of his walking stick became fish, and fallen leaves thrown into the sky became birds. Last of all, the Chief made all the other creatures on Earth.

God's creation. Creationists believe our universe is the work of God, a divine creator. Everything that has ever happened, from the birth of stars to the creation of human life, is part of God's plan for the cosmos.

WORD ORIGINS

Astronomy: The word *astronomy* combines two ancient Greek words, *astron* (star) and *nemein* (to name). Astronomy is the science of naming and understanding the stars.

• THE COSMIC CALENDAR •

When astronomers describe space, they talk about trillions of stars, billions of galaxies, and millions of years of creation. Astronomer Carl Sagan developed a "cosmic calendar" to illustrate how big these numbers really are. To understand the calendar, imagine that all of history is shrunk into a single year. On January 1st, the universe was created. December 31st, at midnight, is life today—right now.

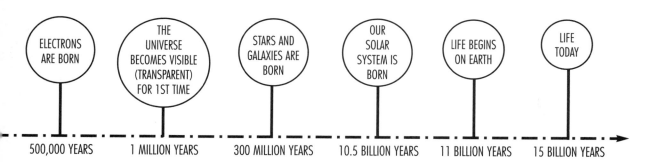

ELECTRONS ARE BORN	THE UNIVERSE BECOMES VISIBLE (TRANSPARENT) FOR 1ST TIME	STARS AND GALAXIES ARE BORN	OUR SOLAR SYSTEM IS BORN	LIFE BEGINS ON EARTH	LIFE TODAY
500,000 YEARS	1 MILLION YEARS	300 MILLION YEARS	10.5 BILLION YEARS	11 BILLION YEARS	15 BILLION YEARS

January 1	origin of the universe (the Big Bang)
May 1	origin of the Milky Way galaxy
September 9	origin of our solar system
September 14	origin of the Earth
September 25	origin of life on Earth
December 24	first dinosaurs
December 31, 10:30 P.M.	first humans
December 31, 11:59:35 P.M.	first cities
December 31, 11:59:59 P.M.	first use of science
January 1, 00:00:01 A.M.	first exploration of space

Of course, our universe is fifteen billion instead of one year old, but this calendar reveals how new we humans are and how little time we've had to understand and explore the space around us.

SPACE PIONEERS

Carl Sagan (1934–96) was fascinated by the stars and the possibility of alien life beyond Earth. Both an astronomer and a biologist, he was one of the founders of America's space program. Sagan helped train the *Apollo* astronauts for their Moon missions and send space probes to Venus, Mars, Jupiter, Saturn, Uranus, and Neptune. He spent much of his life trying to make contact with extraterrestrial life.

Sagan was most famous, however, for making space science popular with ordinary people. He cofounded the Planetary Society, the world's largest space organization, and wrote *Cosmos*, which became the most popular science book ever. A television version of *Cosmos* has been seen by 500 million people around the globe.

CARL SAGAN

• ASTROLOGY VERSUS ASTRONOMY •

People often confuse astrology with astronomy because the words are similar and both involve studying the stars—but the two are very different. *Astronomy* is the science of space and is devoted to understanding the laws of the universe and its trillions of stars and planets. *Astrology* is the belief that the motion of the planets and stars controls our destiny, based upon where and when each of us was born.

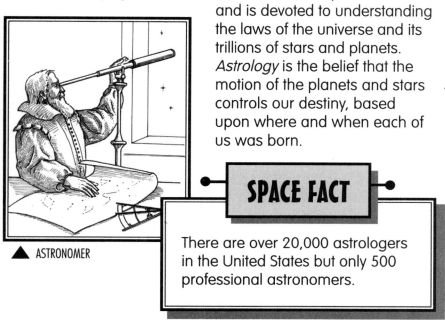

▲ ASTRONOMER

ASTROLOGER ▲

SPACE FACT

There are over 20,000 astrologers in the United States but only 500 professional astronomers.

• WHERE DOES SPACE BEGIN? •

When people use the word "space," they can mean a lot of different things. Space can be any wide open area. Where you are right now is your *personal space*. You leave your car in a *parking space*. You can even talk about the *space* between your ears! But what is "space," really? The space astronomers refer to is *outer space*, a place outside the bounds of the Earth.

SPACE JARGON

Light-year: 5.9 trillion miles, the distance light travels in one Earth year. (The speed of light is 186,000 miles per second.)

• HOW BIG IS THE UNIVERSE? •

It's hard to imagine how big the universe really is. For one thing, the universe is expanding, which means it's getting bigger all the time! It's currently believed to be about fifteen billion *light-years* across, which means that light takes fifteen billion years to travel from one end to the other, moving at 186,000 miles per second. But how big is that? Let's look at the distances to closer, more familiar objects for comparison:

Earth to Moon	230,000 miles
Earth to Sun	93 million miles
Sun to closest star, Alpha Centauri	4.2 light-years, or 25 trillion miles
Sun to center of the Milky Way	30,000 light-years
Milky Way to closest galaxy, the small Magellanic Cloud	196,000 light-years
Milky Way to Andromeda Galaxy	2.2 million light-years
Milky Way to Whirlpool Galaxy	37 million light-years
Milky Way to Cartwheel Galaxy	500 million light-years
Earth to furthest galaxies seen	10 billion light-years
Diameter of the entire universe	15 billion light-years

• TWELVE UNIVERSAL LAWS •

Even though our universe is evolving, some things about it will never change. These are called Universal Laws.

1. The speed of light: Light travels at a speed of 186,000 miles per second. It is impossible for anything to move faster than the speed of light. It is the universe's speed limit.

2. Kepler's first law of planetary motion: Planets travel in elliptical orbits with their sun at one of the two focal points (a circle has one center point, an ellipse has two focal points).

3. Kepler's second law of planetary motion: A planet moves faster when it is closer to its sun, and orbits slower when it is farther away.

SPACE FACT

The unchanging universe. Even though the universe's countless stars and galaxies are constantly being born and dying, the total amount of mass and energy in the universe has never changed. Everything that exists today was compressed into the Big Bang and has been expanding and cooling ever since.

SPACE PIONEERS

Johannes Kepler's insights into the laws of the universe helped create the science of astronomy. In some ways, Kepler (1571–1630) was very mistaken about the order of things: He believed that the Sun and the other planets revolved around the Earth. But he was a brilliant mathematician, and, after years of calculating the motion of the planets, he realized that they traveled in elliptical orbits instead of perfect circles.

JOHANNES KEPLER

4. Kepler's third law of planetary motion: The distance that a planet is from its sun and the time it takes to complete one orbit always have the same proportion to each other.

5. Newton's first law of planetary motion: Everything remains at rest or in motion until moved by an external force (such as wind or gravity).

6. Newton's second law of planetary motion: When an object is moved by an external force, it moves at the same speed and in the same direction as the force.

7. Newton's third law of planetary motion: Every action has an equal, opposite reaction.

8. Newton's first law of gravity: Every particle attracts every other particle.

SPACE PIONEERS

Isaac Newton (1642–1727) was one of the greatest scientific geniuses of all time. Among other discoveries, he proved that white light is the combination of all colors in the visible spectrum. He invented calculus, a kind of math very useful for complex calculations. Most important, he realized that the same gravity that controlled life on Earth worked throughout the universe and that it was this force that kept the planets revolving around the Sun.

ISAAC NEWTON

9. Newton's second law of gravity: The power of attraction is based on the size of the particles and the distance between them.

10. Einstein's general theory of relativity: Gravity (motion) and speed of motion (time) are two forces that cannot be separated. This is called "space-time."

SPACE PIONEERS

Albert Einstein (1879–1955) is probably the most famous scientist who ever lived. His theories of relativity (see " Twelve Universal Laws" on page 12) predicted that motion and time are connected and that time slows down as a person or an object speeds up. According to this theory, time would almost stop for a person moving near the speed of light, and he or she would not age at all! Today's astronomers and physicists, using sophisticated new equipment, are discovering that Einstein's amazing theories are true.

ALBERT EINSTEIN

11. Einstein's special theory of relativity: Time moves more slowly for someone in motion than for someone standing still.

12. Hubble's law: The farther a galaxy is from our own, the faster it is moving away from us (as the universe expands).

SPACE PIONEERS

Edwin Hubble (1889–1953) didn't plan to be an astronomer. Instead, he wanted to play football, but his mother disapproved. So Hubble enrolled in Oxford University in England and began to study the stars. He worked at Mount Wilson Observatory, the world's largest telescope (at that time). Hubble made dramatic discoveries: He proved that the universe was filled with galaxies, stretching billions of light-years beyond the Milky Way. He also discovered the universe was expanding, which led to the Big Bang theory. Hubble found the key to the origin of our universe.

EDWIN HUBBLE

• OUR TEN-DIMENSIONAL UNIVERSE •

We think of ourselves as living in a three-dimensional world, but astrophysicists have discovered that our universe is, in fact, a ten-dimensional place. Where are the extra dimensions?

First, let's consider the dimensions we are familiar with. The first dimension is any point in space, a single dot without reference to anything else. The second dimension exists on a flat plane, like a line drawn on a piece of paper. The third dimension adds depth, creating the front-to-back, side-to-side, up-and-down world we know from everyday experience. The fourth dimension adds time to the equation, which Einstein proved could not be separated from space.

As physicists began to unlock the subatomic particles that make up the universe, however, they realized that there are more dimensions existing at a microscopic level—too small to be seen by the human eye. Understanding where particles exist in space could require as many as six extra dimensions!

• SPACE JARGON: A UNIVERSAL PRIMER •

The universe: All known matter and energy, believed to have begun from a single point fifteen billion years ago and released through a gigantic explosion known as the Big Bang.

Supercluster: A collection of galaxies bound together by mutual gravity. A single supercluster may contain millions of individual galaxies.

Galaxy: A vast collection of stars bound together by gravity and orbiting about a core. Galaxies can contain millions or billions of individual stars.

Cluster: A loose collection of stars within a cloud of interstellar gas and dust. Clusters can hold dozens or thousands of stars.

Constellation: A series of stars forming figures or shapes in the sky. The eighty-eight constellations are artificial groupings; their stars are not bound together by mutual gravity.

Heliopause: The boundary between the solar system and deep space. At this point, wind heated by the Sun meets the cold wind of interstellar space.

Solar System: The region in space influenced by a single star's gravity. A solar system can extend far beyond its planets to vast clouds of microscopic particles.

Star: Gaseous bodies releasing heat and energy through thermonuclear reactions. Stars vary in size and density and change their output throughout their lives.

Planet: A body orbiting about a star. Our solar system has nine known planets. How many other planets exist throughout the universe is unknown.

Moon: A body orbiting a planet. Some planets have no moons, while others have dozens.

Asteroid: Minor planets orbiting a sun. Most asteroids are small, irregularly shaped, rocky bodies left over from a solar system's formation.

Comet: Icy bodies orbiting a sun. Comets heat up as their elliptical orbits bring them closer to a star, releasing a long tail of slush and vapor particles into space.

Meteor: A chunk of space debris entering a planet's atmosphere. A meteor can range from the size of a grain of sand to miles in diameter.

Planetesimal: Small clumps of space matter (sometimes called asteroids) left over from the formation of the planets. Planetesimals can be as large as 60 miles wide.

Meteorite: A meteor large enough to pass through a planet's atmosphere and impact the planet's surface.

Micrometeoroid: Tiny grains of space dust entering a planet's atmosphere.

• GALAXIES •

WORD ORIGINS

Milky Way: The name "Milky Way" comes from the Greek *galaxias,* meaning "milky." The broad band of stars stretching across the night sky is like a stream of milk against the blackness of space.

Three hundred million years after the Big Bang, gravity pulled vast clouds of space particles into tighter clumps. From these furnaces of dust and gas, the stars were born. Billions of stars orbiting about a central core form each of the universe's galaxies. There are four main types of galaxies: spiral (type S), barred spiral (type SB), elliptical (type E), and irregular (type I). Galaxies are like fingerprints: No two are exactly alike.

Our own galaxy, the Milky Way, is a spiral galaxy, but we see its stars as a broad line across the sky instead of as a spiral. We see the Milky Way along its edge because we are inside it.

• SUPERCLUSTERS •

Gravity does more than bind stars together into galaxies. Our Milky Way is but a small dot on the edge of a constellation of millions of galaxies called the Local Supercluster. And space is much larger than that: Our supercluster is just one of many superclusters, all orbiting about some unknown point in the universe!

A SPIRAL GALAXY AS SEEN FROM EDGE ON ▲

• STARS •

The skies overhead are filled with stars, some near and bright, some far away and very dim. The universe has many different types of stars. They range in surface temperature from 3,000 to 100,000 degrees Fahrenheit (°F). The color of a star reveals how hot it is. Hot stars are blue, and cool stars are red.

• A STAR GUIDE •

Black dwarf: A white dwarf that has become black after burning up all its fuel.

Blue giant: A very large, hot, bright star.

Brown dwarf: A failed star larger than a planet but unable to produce thermonuclear reactions and shine.

Dwarf star: A small star that glows very dimly.

17

Orange giant: A large star with medium-cool surface temperature.

Pulsating star: A star that varies in brightness.

Red dwarf: A small, dim star with low temperature.

Red giant: A large star with low surface temperature.

White dwarf: A small, cold star at the end of its life cycle.

White supergiant: A very large, medium-hot, bright star.

Yellow star: An ordinary star of medium temperature, such as our Sun. Yellow stars emit white light but can appear to be yellow when viewed from a planet's surface.

• THE CLOSEST STARS •

Star	Constellation	Type of star	Distance from Earth
Sun	—	yellow	93 million miles
Alpha Centauri	Centaurus	yellow-white	4.3 light-years
Barnard's Star	Ophiuchus	red dwarf	5.9 light-years
Wolf 359	Leo	red dwarf	7.6 light-years
Lalanda 21185	Ursa Major	red dwarf	8.1 light-years
Luyten 726-8	Cetus	red dwarf	8.4 light-years
Sirius	Canis Major	blue-white	8.8 light-years

• THE BRIGHTEST STARS •

Star	Constellation	Type of star	Distance from Earth
Sun	—	yellow	93 million miles
Sirius	Canis Major	blue-white	8.8 light-years
Canopus	Carina	white supergiant	74 light-years
Arcturus	Bootes	orange giant	36 light-years
Alpha Centauri	Centaurus	yellow-white	4.3 light-years
Vega	Lyra	blue-white	26 light-years
Capella	Auriga	yellow giant	42 light-years

• THE HOTTEST OF STARS •

In October 1997, astronomers announced the discovery of what may be the biggest and brightest star in the universe, nicknamed the "Pistol Star" (after the pistol-shaped nebula that surrounds it). The Pistol Star is ten million times more powerful than our Sun—so large that, in our solar system, it would stretch beyond the orbit of Mars. Every six seconds, it emits as much energy as our Sun puts out in an entire year.

Despite its size and brightness, the Pistol Star remains invisible to Earth's optical telescopes because of an obscuring cloud of interstellar dust. To find the star, astronomers searched the skies with the Hubble Space Telescope's Near-Infrared Camera, which can peer through dark clouds of gas and dust to find sources of heat in the universe.

• MULTIPLE STARS •

Although our solar system has just one star—the Sun—most stars have at least one companion. (If Jupiter had been larger, its gas atmosphere might have ignited and become a second star in our solar system.) A system with two stars is called a *binary star system*. A system with more than two stars is called a *multiple star system*.

In binary or multiple star systems, the mutual gravity of the orbiting stars has a powerful effect on each star's life-and-death sequence. Most star systems have a dominant and a lesser star. When two stars are closest in their mutual orbits, the hotter star draws matter off the cooler one, gaining in size and power. Multiple stars can trade matter back and forth several times over the course of their lives.

• THE FATE OF STARS •

Stars vary in size, ranging from one-tenth the size of the Sun to 100 times larger. The life span of a star—how long it radiates heat and light, and what happens after its fuel is gone—depends on its size at birth.

Our Sun is a fairly ordinary yellow star. After it has burned up all its remaining fuel (about five billion years from now), it will expand in size to become a red giant, stretching beyond the orbit of Mars. After the remaining helium burns off, the Sun's outer layers will escape into space, leaving a small white dwarf.

A star ten times more massive than our Sun will expand to become a supergiant. After its gases are depleted, its core will collapse, leaving a tiny neutron star or spinning pulsar. A star thirty to fifty times more massive than the Sun will also become a supergiant. But because it is so large it will cause a supernova—a giant explosion collapsing the core with so much force that the star reduces in size to a singularity (a black hole).

Our Solar System

A solar system is more than a sun and its planets; it's anything and everything that revolves around a star. Our own solar system contains the Sun, nine planets and their moons, and thousands of asteroids and comets. But the solar system doesn't stop there. Stretching far off into space is a collection of orbiting ice particles called the Oort Cloud which extends our solar system halfway to the nearest star, Proxima Centauri—almost 4 light-years, or 23.6 trillion miles, into space!

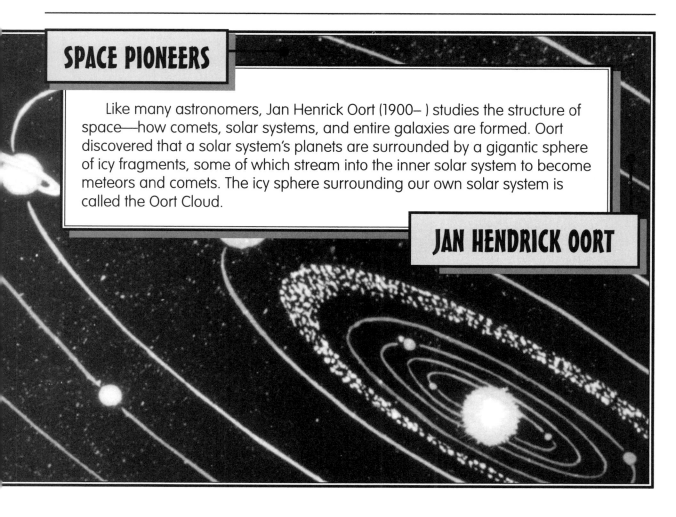

SPACE PIONEERS

Like many astronomers, Jan Henrick Oort (1900–) studies the structure of space—how comets, solar systems, and entire galaxies are formed. Oort discovered that a solar system's planets are surrounded by a gigantic sphere of icy fragments, some of which stream into the inner solar system to become meteors and comets. The icy sphere surrounding our own solar system is called the Oort Cloud.

JAN HENDRICK OORT

• THE SUN •

The Milky Way Galaxy is approximately 100,000 light-years wide and 20,000 light-years thick. Our star, the Sun, lies about 30,000 light-years (or two-thirds of the way) outward from the center, along the outer edge of one of the spiraling arms. Compared to the Milky Way, our Sun is very small. It takes the Sun 220 million years just to complete one orbit of the galaxy. But to us, the Sun is huge. It contains 99.86 percent of all matter in the solar system. (It would take more than 1.3 million Earths to equal its size!)

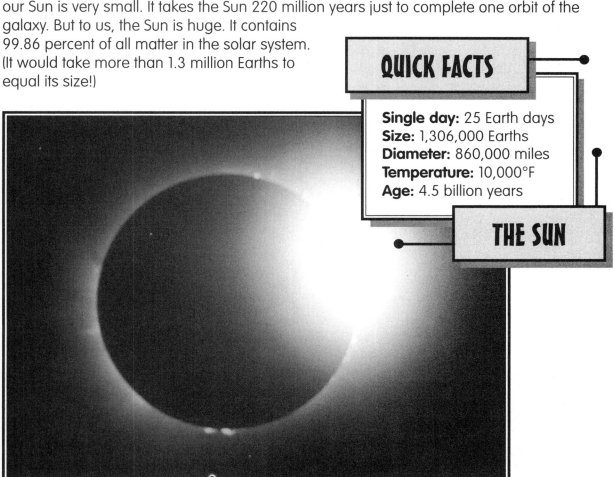

QUICK FACTS

Single day: 25 Earth days
Size: 1,306,000 Earths
Diameter: 860,000 miles
Temperature: 10,000°F
Age: 4.5 billion years

THE SUN

THE SUN NEAR TOTAL ECLIPSE ▲

Our Sun is a very ordinary star in the middle of its life cycle. Astronomers in other solar systems would not know there was anything special about it. But the Sun is responsible for all life on Earth. It produced particles that formed our atmosphere. It heats our planet and allows us to live. Without our Sun, our world would be a cold, dark, and lifeless place.

SPACE PIONEERS

Nicolaus Copernicus (1473–1543) was a shy student who was fascinated by mathematics, art, astronomy, and medicine. People of his day believed the Sun, the Moon, and the other planets revolved around the Earth, but Copernicus's astronomical observations showed this to be untrue. He put his ideas into a manuscript called *De revolutionibus orbium coelestium (Concerning the Revolution of the Heavenly Spheres)*. Because religious leaders believed the Earth was the center of the universe, however, his writings remained unpublished until after his death.

NICOLAUS COPERNICUS

• THE SUN QUAKES, TOO •

The energy we get from our Sun comes from powerful nuclear reactions deep inside its core; light comes from the upper surfaces, the photosphere and chromosphere. These layers are always in motion, with some areas brighter and others darker (what we call "sunspots"). Sunspots sometimes erupt into huge solar flares, streams of superheated gas leaping hundreds of thousands of miles into space.

Now astronomers have discovered that solar flares produce sunquakes inside the Sun's interior, just like earthquakes here on Earth—only many times more powerful. One such quake measured 11.3 on the Richter scale, 40,000 times more powerful than the huge earthquake that destroyed San Francisco in 1906. In a single sunquake, enough energy is released to power the entire United States for twenty years.

SOLAR FLARES CAN LEAP HUNDREDS OF THOUSANDS OF MILES INTO SPACE ▲

• THE PLANETS •

Although no two planets are exactly alike, all planets discovered so far can be grouped into two categories: terrestrial planets and gas giants.

When a solar system begins to form, the new star sends streams of gas, dust, and other particles outward into space. The lightest materials—gases such as hydrogen and helium—travel farther leaving clouds of heavier particles closer to the Sun. As the star cools, planets begin to form out of the orbiting material. Outer planets are made largely of gas, and inner planets mostly of heavier, rocky materials. This explains why our solar system has terrestrial, earthlike planets closer to the Sun and gas giants deeper in space.

Pluto, the farthest planet from our Sun, is not a gas giant—but Pluto's orbit is unlike any other in the solar system, and Pluto may have been captured by our Sun's gravity after the formation of the other planets (see page 36).

A FAMILY PORTRAIT OF PLANETS (PLUTO NOT SHOWN)

THE PLANETS: TERRESTRIAL OR GAS GIANT?

Mercury	terrestrial	**Mars**	terrestrial	**Uranus**	gas giant
Venus	terrestrial	**Jupiter**	gas giant	**Neptune**	gas giant
Earth	terrestrial	**Saturn**	gas giant	**Pluto**	terrestrial

• HOW THE PLANETS GOT THEIR NAMES •

• PLANET •	• MYTHOLOGY •	• REALITY •
Mercury	In Roman myth, Mercury was Jupiter's messenger—so fast that he had wings on his heels.	Mercury is the planet with the fastest orbit around the Sun. A year on Mercury lasts only 88 Earth days.
Venus	Venus was the Roman goddess of love, famous for her fiery temper.	Venus's stormy cloud cover gives it the hottest surface temperature in the solar system (882°F).
Earth	In Greek mythology, Gaia (or Earth) was considered the goddess of our planet, or Mother Earth.	Although life originated in our planet's oceans, we call ourselves Earth because that is where we live—on the land.
Mars	Mars was the Roman god of war.	The Red Planet (so called because its soil and even the sky are tinted red) looked much more warlike than the calm, blue Earth.
Jupiter	Jupiter was the Roman king of the gods.	Jupiter is the largest planet in the solar system (almost large enough to be a second sun), a king among worlds.

Saturn	Saturn was king of the Titans (what the gods were called before they became gods). He was replaced by Jupiter.	If Jupiter didn't exist, Saturn would be the largest of the planets.
Uranus	Uranus was the Roman god of civilization and culture.	Even though Uranus is a gas giant, the planet appears blue, very much like the civilized Earth.
Neptune	Neptune was the Roman god of the seas.	Neptune is a blue-colored planet, covered with gas instead of earth-like seas.
Pluto	Pluto was the Roman god of the underworld, the home of the dead. He was also called Hades, which means "the invisible."	Pluto the planet is a cold, remote world, almost invisible to earth-based telescopes.

• WHY DO SOME PLANETS HAVE RINGS? •

Of the nine known planets in our solar system, Saturn, Jupiter, Uranus, and Neptune have orbiting rings, and the remaining five do not. Astronomers trying to unravel the mystery of what causes ring formation have sent space probes to study these rings in closer detail.

The rings are made up of millions of pieces of ice, dust, and rocks, ranging in size from a few inches to several feet in diameter. Since each of the ringed planets is a gas giant, astronomers believe the rings are pieces of moons that never formed due to these planets' strong gravitational pull. Only those clouds of dust and ice far enough away from each planet were able to form into orbiting moons. For more information on planetary ring formation, visit: http://newproducts.jpl.nasa.gov/saturn/faq.html

PLANETARY RINGS ▲

• RELATIVE GRAVITY •

All bodies in the solar system have different gravitational pulls. The Moon's gravity is only one-sixth as strong as Earth's, which means that an astronaut standing on the Moon can jump six times higher than at home. Mars has one-third Earth's gravity, while Jupiter's gravity is 2.34 times stronger (which would make moving about on Jupiter's surface almost impossible).

Humans are perfectly adapted to Earth's gravity. We neither float above the ground nor feel weighted down as we move about the planet's surface. A person weighing 100 pounds on Earth would weigh only 17 pounds on the Moon, but 234 pounds on Jupiter! To see what you would weigh on different planets, visit:
http://www.exploratorium.edu/ronh/weight/index.html

• MERCURY: A PLANET THAT FREEZES AND BURNS •

No planet suffers more radical temperature changes than Mercury, the world nearest our Sun. The smallest planet circling the *ecliptic plane*, it is a world without atmosphere. It is lifeless and covered with ancient craters. As Mercury rotates, the temperature can rise to 800°F during the day and drop to -275°F each night. It is a world of fire and ice.

Because it is so near the Sun, Mercury can actually have two sunrises in a single day. How? The first sunrise occurs when the Sun rises in the early morning, just as on Earth. The second sunrise can occur when Mercury's orbit is nearest the Sun. Because the planet rotates so slowly (a

SPACE JARGON

Ecliptic plane: The narrow band of space in which our solar system's planets orbit the Sun. Only Pluto, with an eccentric orbit that sometimes brings it closer than Neptune to the Sun, orbits above and below the ecliptic plane.

Mercury year is only slightly longer than a single Mercury day!), the Sun can appear to dip below the horizon and then rise again before setting for the night. For further information and images of Mercury, visit: http://nssdc.gsfc.nasa.gov/planetary/planets/mercurypage.html

WORD ORIGINS

Mercurial: To be called "mercurial" suggests that you change your mood very quickly. Ancient astronomers believed that, since Mercury was closest to the Sun, those under the planet's influence would experience rapid changes of mood and attitude.

QUICK FACTS

Distance from Sun: 36,000,000 miles
Single year: 88 Earth days
Single day: 59 Earth days
Size: 0.056 Earth
Diameter: 3,030 miles
Moons: 0
Temperature: -275°F to 800°F

MERCURY

• VENUS: A WORLD GONE HORRIBLY WRONG •

Venus is often called Earth's "sister planet," because it is almost the same size as our world and orbits the Sun at a similar rate. Millions of years ago, Venus and Earth may have looked very alike— peaceful blue-water worlds with rocky land masses. But something on Venus went very, very wrong. Carbon dioxide (the same gas spewed by automobile exhaust) built up in the atmosphere, trapping heat beneath a heavy cloud

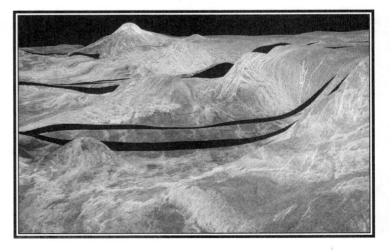

cover. As more and more heat built up, surface temperatures rose to a hellish 870°F. Scientists call this phenomenon the "greenhouse effect."

The *Magellan* spacecraft, launched in 1989, used radar to peer through Venus's thick cloud cover, sending back images of nearly 99 percent of the planet's surface. Venus was revealed as a world of gigantic volcanoes, canyons, and craters. All oceans on the planet's surface have long since boiled off into the dense cloud layers, which rain deadly sulfuric acid instead of water. Venus is a planet no astronaut can ever visit. For further information and images of Venus, visit: http://nssdc.gsfc.nasa.gov/planetary/planets/venuspage.html

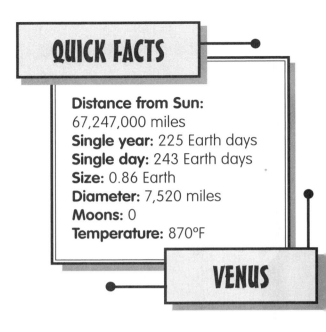

QUICK FACTS

Distance from Sun: 67,247,000 miles
Single year: 225 Earth days
Single day: 243 Earth days
Size: 0.86 Earth
Diameter: 7,520 miles
Moons: 0
Temperature: 870°F

VENUS

• EARTH: OUR HOME WORLD •

As far as we know, Earth is the only planet in the solar system (or the entire universe) capable of supporting life. It is the only planet with a thick atmosphere and liquid water on its surface, factors scientists believe may be necessary for the

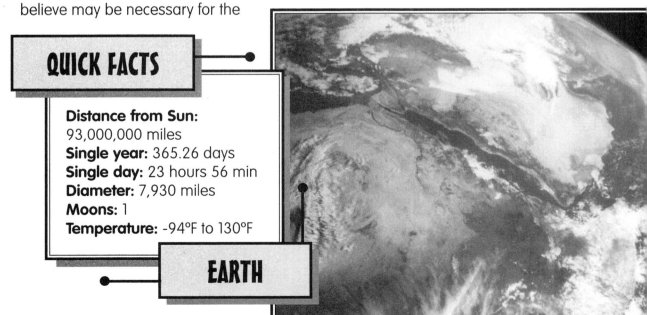

QUICK FACTS

Distance from Sun: 93,000,000 miles
Single year: 365.26 days
Single day: 23 hours 56 min
Diameter: 7,930 miles
Moons: 1
Temperature: -94°F to 130°F

EARTH

development of organic molecules (Jupiter's moon Europa may also harbor an ocean under its surface of ice; it is the second most likely candidate for a life-sustaining world in our solar system). Earth's orbit is fairly circular, so our planet experiences neither extreme changes in temperature nor intense gravitational upheaval caused by the Sun.

All in all, ours is a peaceful world floating in a violent and deadly universe. For further information and images of Earth, visit: http://nssdc.gsfc.nasa.gov/planetary/planets/earthpage.html

• EARTH'S ATMOSPHERE •

Earth's atmosphere has many different layers; the higher you go, the thinner the air. Fifty miles up, Earth's atmosphere ends. That is where outer space begins.

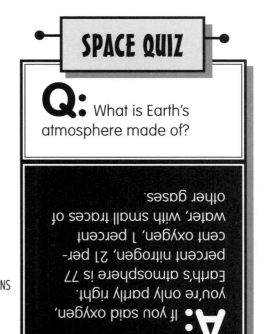

EXOSPHERE	ABOVE 400 MILES	INTERPLANETARY SPACECRAFT
THERMOSPHERE	50–400 MILES	SPACE SHUTTLES SATELLITES METEORS AURORA
MESOSPHERE	30–50 MILES	HIGH-ALTITUDE AIRCRAFT
STRATOSPHERE	10–30 MILES	AIRPLANES WEATHER BALLOONS CLOUDS
TROPOSPHERE	6–10 MILES	HELICOPTERS CLOUDS KITES

SPACE QUIZ

Q: What is Earth's atmosphere made of?

A: If you said oxygen, you're only partly right. Earth's atmosphere is 77 percent nitrogen, 21 percent oxygen, 1 percent water, with small traces of other gases.

• DOES EACH DAY SEEM A LITTLE LONGER? . . . IT IS! •

Four billion years ago, when the Earth was young, a single day lasted only eight hours. Today, a full rotation takes twenty-four hours. Why is the Earth spinning more slowly than in the past?

As Earth spins on its axis, tidal friction—the motion of the seas—slows down our planet making each day just a little bit longer. How much longer? Scientists estimate that we may be gaining as much as ten thousandths of a second each day. In another four billion years, a single day could be forty hours long!

• MARS: THE RED PLANET •

Earth's other neighbor in the solar system is the small, rust-covered planet Mars. Rusted (oxidized) iron in Martian soil gives the planet a red appearance. Violent winds blow billowing red dust storms across the planet's surface at hundreds of miles per hour. Even the skies glow reddish pink on Mars, instead of blue. For these reasons, Mars is often called "the Red Planet."

Mars is a place somewhat similar to Earth in important ways. Both planets have four seasons, polar ice caps, stable temperatures, and magnetic iron cores. But the Martian atmosphere is too thin to protect the planet's surface from the Sun's deadly ultraviolet radiation, and the only water remaining on the planet surface is trapped in ice at the poles.

Recent discoveries suggest that Mars may have been much warmer and wetter in the distant past, with flowing rivers and an atmosphere

SPACE QUIZ

Q: Every four years is a "leap year," 366 days long instead of the usual 365. Why?

A: The Earth takes 365¼ days to revolve around the Sun. Our calendar is adjusted every fourth year to account for the extra day.

more hospitable to life. Scientists have sent unmanned probes to Mars to search for traces of life and to seek clues to the evaporation of Mars's atmosphere. For further information and images of Mars, visit: http://nssdc.gsfc.nasa.gov/planetary/planets/marspage.html

• VESTA: THE ASTEROID-MAKER •

Halfway between Mars and Jupiter lies a wide ring of asteroids called the asteroid belt. Astronomers have recently discovered a source for many of these asteroids: a miniplanet called Vesta.

Vesta is a super-asteroid, 330 miles wide, first discovered by German astronomer Wilhelm Olbers in 1807. Using the Hubble Space Telescope, researchers have found a crater 285 miles wide and 8 miles deep carved into Vesta's surface—the result of a gigantic impact with another asteroid a billion or more years ago. Enough material was thrown into space during that collision to account for thousands of smaller orbiting bodies in the asteroid belt.

Over millions of years, many of these asteroids have fallen to Earth. It is fitting that pieces of Vesta should be falling to Earth: Vesta is named after the Roman goddess of the hearth, or home. For further information on the asteroid Vesta, visit: http://nssdc.gsfc.nasa.gov/planetary/text/vesta_pr_970904.txt

QUICK FACTS

Distance from Sun:
141,600,000 miles
Single year: 687 Earth days
Single day: 24 hours 37 min
Diameter: 4,217 miles
Moons: 2
Temperature: -185°F to +77°F

MARS

HALLEY'S COMET ▲

• A FREQUENT VISITOR •

Most of our solar system's asteroids and comets orbit the Sun in regular cycles, just like the planets. Astronomers can predict when individual comets will pass by the Earth and be visible in the skies overhead. The best-known of these regular visitors is probably Halley's comet, which flies by the Earth every seventy-six years.

Halley's comet is named after the astronomer who first predicted its return in 1682, Sir Edmund Halley. Today, scientists can do more than wait for a comet's return: In 1986, the European Space Agency (ESA) launched the *Giotto* probe on a mission to visit Halley's comet. *Giotto* returned pictures of the comet, revealing it to be a giant potato-shaped object, 9 miles long and 5 miles wide, surrounded by a large plume of ice vapor as it streaks through the heavens. For more information on the *Giotto* mission, visit: http://nssdc.gsfc.nasa.gov/planetary/giotto.html

• JUPITER: KING OF THE PLANETS •

Aside from the Sun, Jupiter is the most massive object in the solar system. It is larger than all the other planets combined. (If Jupiter had been sixty times more massive, it may have ignited and become a second sun in our solar system instead of a planet.) Jupiter is a gas giant comprised of multicolored bands of swirling hydrogen, helium, methane, ammonia, and water vapor. Its thick atmosphere, surrounding a solid rocky core only 18,650 miles wide, accounts for 80 percent of the planet's diameter.

Violent winds blow Jupiter's atmosphere in an endless cycle around the planet. West winds reach 110 miles per hour, and east winds reach as much as 270 miles per hour. Where these winds meet, they can create swirls and storms that rage for years. One storm, called "the Great Red Spot" (the red color is probably produced by sulfur broken down by sunlight), has been sighted for more than

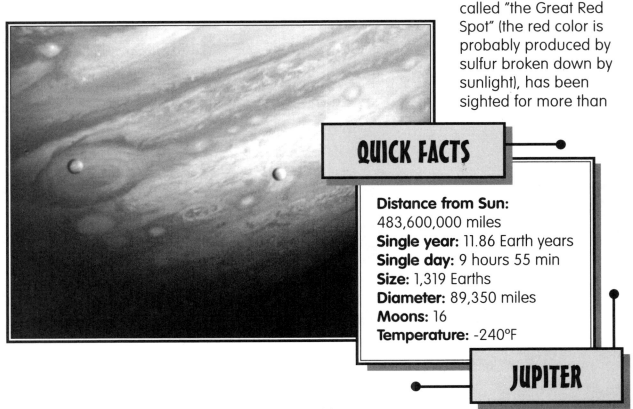

QUICK FACTS

Distance from Sun: 483,600,000 miles
Single year: 11.86 Earth years
Single day: 9 hours 55 min
Size: 1,319 Earths
Diameter: 89,350 miles
Moons: 16
Temperature: -240°F

JUPITER

300 years. This single storm spans over 25,000 miles—three times the diameter of the Earth! For further information and images of Jupiter, visit: http://nssdc.gsfc.nasa.gov/planetary/planets/jupiterpage.html

Spinning at different speeds. A gas giant like Jupiter doesn't rotate the way a terrestrial planet like Earth does. Even though Earth's atmosphere is made up of several different layers, everything rotates at the same speed, 18.5 miles per second. On Jupiter, however, the various layers of gas rotate at different speeds, averaging five hours and fifty minutes for each revolution. The rocky core of the planet rotates more slowly, closer to six hours per orbit.

• SATURN: THE RINGED GIANT •

Saturn is one of four planets in our solar system ringed by orbiting particles of ice, rock, and dust, but it is by far the most remarkable of the "ringed" gas giants. Saturn's rings are very thin, no more than a hundred yards wide. They stretch over vast

A WORLD OF VOLCANOES

We inhabit a solar system filled with volcanoes. Earth's rocky crust is periodically re-formed by new lava flows. Venus shows a history of intense volcanic activity. Mars has the solar system's largest volcano, Olympus Mons, towering 15 miles high (almost four times the size of Earth's largest volcanoes). But which of these planets is the most volcanic place in the solar system? None. Jupiter's little moon Io holds that record—it is a world covered by volcanoes in near-constant eruption. For more information on Io, visit: http://www.jpl.nasa.gov/galileo/io

distances, starting 4,300 miles above the planet's atmosphere and reaching some 46,000 miles into space.

Like Jupiter, Saturn has a turbulent atmosphere with swirling storms that can rage for hundreds of years. Saturn features a "Great Red Spot," too (although this storm is only one-fourth the size of Jupiter's).

Saturn is the second-largest planet in the solar system. Among its many wonders is the moon Titan, one of only three terrestrial worlds in the solar system supporting a thick atmosphere. (Earth and Venus are the others.) Astronomers are uncertain whether Titan is covered by oceans, land, or ice. For further information and images of Saturn, visit: http://nssdc.gsfc.nasa.gov/planetary/planets/saturnpage.html

QUICK FACTS

Distance from Sun: 886,000,000 miles
Single year: 29.5 Earth years
Single day: 10 hours 40 min
Size: 744 Earths
Diameter: 74,900 miles
Moons: 18
Temperature: -292°F

SATURN

• URANUS: A WORLD ON ITS SIDE •

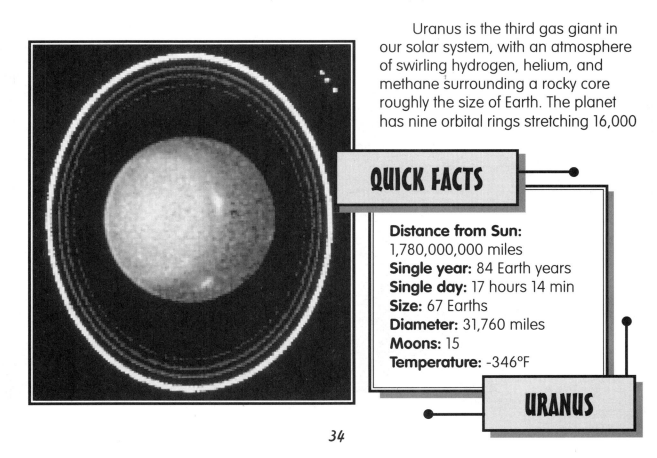

Uranus is the third gas giant in our solar system, with an atmosphere of swirling hydrogen, helium, and methane surrounding a rocky core roughly the size of Earth. The planet has nine orbital rings stretching 16,000

QUICK FACTS

Distance from Sun: 1,780,000,000 miles
Single year: 84 Earth years
Single day: 17 hours 14 min
Size: 67 Earths
Diameter: 31,760 miles
Moons: 15
Temperature: -346°F

URANUS

miles into space. Unlike Jupiter's and Saturn's rings, however (which are largely water ice), Uranus's rings contain mysterious dark materials that astronomers are eager to study further.

Most unusual about Uranus is the tilt of the planet. Uranus is a world on its side, orbiting the Sun at an angle so severe that its north pole lies below the point of Earth's equator. Astronomers believe that Uranus was struck by a large meteor at some period in the past and knocked sideways into its current position. In order to dislodge the giant planet, that meteor would have to have been at least half the size of the Earth. (If a similar-size meteor were to strike Earth, our planet would be pulverized!)

Some of Uranus's moons show evidence of cataclysms of their own. Miranda, the smallest and nearest of the planet's major moons, looks like a world smashed into pieces and clumped back together. Its surface is covered by rocky terrain that changes directions abruptly, like jigsaw pieces that don't quite fit together. For more information and images of Uranus, visit: http://nssdc.gsfc.nasa.gov/planetary/planets/uranuspage.html

• NEPTUNE: THE LAST GIANT •

Neptune is a gas giant similar in size to Uranus, with four orbital rings and a thick atmosphere rich in hydrogen and helium. Surrounding its rocky core is a deep ocean of water, methane, and ammonia. Neptune's chemistry gives it a water-blue appearance, but

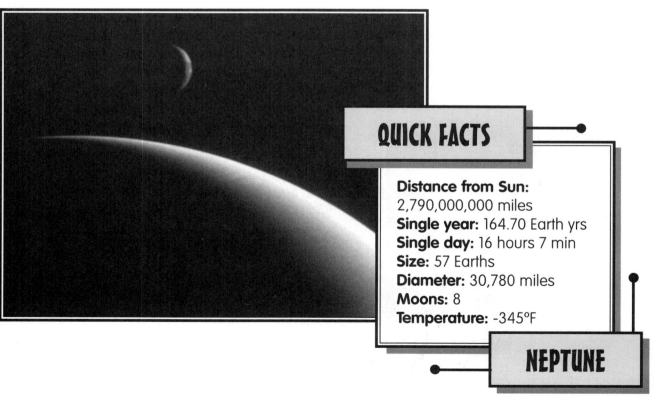

QUICK FACTS

Distance from Sun: 2,790,000,000 miles
Single year: 164.70 Earth yrs
Single day: 16 hours 7 min
Size: 57 Earths
Diameter: 30,780 miles
Moons: 8
Temperature: -345°F

NEPTUNE

it is a frozen world quite unlike our planet's placid blue oceans, with a surface temperature far colder than Earth's.

The raging wind currents that churn Neptune's atmosphere blow faster than anywhere else in the solar system—as fast as 1,250 miles per hour. Like the other gas giants, Neptune appears to feature "permanent" storm systems, including an Earth-size hurricane known as the "Great Dark Spot."

Neptune's moon Triton is the coldest world in the solar system, with temperatures as low as -391°F. Triton is so cold that when volcanoes erupt (probably due to the stresses caused by Neptune's gravitational pull), geysers spout frozen nitrogen instead of molten lava into the air. For further information and images of Neptune, visit: http://nssdc.gsfc.nasa.gov/planetary/planets/neptunepage.html

• PLUTO AND CHARON: A DOUBLE PLANET •

The outermost of our solar system's planets is Pluto, a tiny, icy world smaller than Earth's Moon. Alone among the planets, Pluto orbits the Sun at a tilt, outside the ecliptic plane. Astronomers theorize that Pluto may be a world that was captured by our solar system's gravity after the formation of the other planets.

Pluto's moon, Charon, compared to the size of its planet, is the largest satellite in the solar system. How large is Charon? It is nearly half the size of Pluto. Earth's Moon, by comparison, is only about a quarter the size of our planet.

QUICK FACTS

Distance from Sun:
3,700,000,000 miles
Single year: 248.54 Earth yrs
Single day: 6 days 9 hours
Diameter: 1,420 miles
Temperature: -364°F

PLUTO

Distance from Sun:
3,700,000,000 miles
Distance to Pluto: 12,204 mi
Single year: 248.54 Earth yrs
Single day: 6 days 9 hours
Diameter: 741 miles
Temperature: -364°F

CHARON

Some astronomers believe Pluto and Charon are really "double planets" orbiting each other (every 6.4 days), instead of a planet and its moon.

Pluto and Charon orbit so closely together that they have locked in rotation—the same sides always facing each other. A person standing on Pluto's icy surface would see Charon floating motionless in the sky. The moon never rises or sets. For further information and images of Pluto and Charon, visit:
http://nssdc.gsfc.nasa.gov/planetary/planets/plutopage.html

• MYSTERIOUS PLANETS •

Astronomers believe that most stars have planets, but because they are so far away seeing these other worlds has been impossible. In 1995, however, using sophisticated new equipment, astronomers discovered the first planets outside our solar system. They are mysterious new worlds.

The first planet discovered orbits 51 Pegasi, a star in the constellation Pegasus, 50 light-years away. It is a large gas giant half the size of Jupiter. Amazingly, though, instead of being far away from its sun (like the gas giants in our solar system), this planet orbits only five million miles from 51 Pegasi—seven times closer than Mercury is to our Sun. On this world, a year is only four days long!

Two other planets, orbiting 70 Virginis (59 light-years away) and HD 114762 (91 light-years away) are stranger still. Although these gas giants orbit farther away from their stars, they move in oval instead of circular orbits. (All planets move in elliptical orbits, but most orbits are almost a perfect circle.) Sometimes these planets are very close to their suns, and sometimes they are very, very far away. There would be no mistaking summer and winter on these worlds.

In all, more than a dozen new worlds have been discovered orbiting faraway stars. During just a few short years, astronomers have cataloged more planets outside our solar system than in it!

• THE SEARCH FOR PLANET X •

There may be an undiscovered planet within our own solar system. Astronomers calculating the orbits of Neptune and Uranus have detected a gravitational disturbance that can't be accounted for by the pull of the remaining planets. For many years before the discovery of Pluto, scientists believed a ninth planet caused these irregularities, but after Pluto and its moon, Charon, were discovered, they were shown to be a thousand times too small to account for the gravitational disturbance. Our solar system may have a tenth planet—which, until found, is called "Planet X."

Astronomers believe that Planet X, if it does exist, might lie as far as 15 billion miles beyond the Sun, orbiting only once every thousand years! It may be a long time before Planet X comes close enough to the other planets to be detected.

If astronomers succeed in finding Planet X, what should we call it? The most likely choice might be "Vulcan"—but not after Mr. Spock, the popular *Star Trek* hero from a planet of that name. All of our solar system's planets are named after the gods of ancient Roman mythology, and Jupiter's two sons were named Mars and Vulcan.

• MANY, MANY MOONS •

Most planets have enough gravity to collect small orbiting bodies of their own, behaving like miniature solar systems. In fact, if you looked into space on some planets, you would see a sky practically filled with moons!

• PLANET •	• MOONS •	• NAMES •			
Mercury	0	—			
Venus	0	—			
Earth	1	The Moon			
Mars	2	Phobos	Deimos		
Jupiter	16	Callitsto	Amalthea	Sinope	Leda
		Europa	Himalia	Carme	Adrastea
		Ganymede	Elara	Lysithea	Thebe
		Io	Pasiphae	Ananke	Metis
Saturn	18	Titan	Enceladus	Epimetheus	Prometheus
		Iapetus	Mimas	Atlas	Telesto
		Rhea	Hyperion	Calypso	Pan
		Dione	Phoebe	Helene	
		Tethys	Janus	Pandora	
Uranus	15	Oberon	Miranda	Cordelia	Phelia
		Titania	Puck	Cressida	Portia
		Ariel	Belinda	Desdemona	Rosalind
		Umbriel	Bianca	Juliet	
Neptune	8	Triton	Despoina	Larissa	Proteus
		Nereid	Galatea	Naiad	Thalassa
Pluto	1	Charon			

All our solar system's moons are named after famous characters in mythology and literature, but in fact astronomer's who discover a new moon or star can name it anything they prefer. (It could even be named after you!) Before a new name becomes official, however, it must be certified by the International Astronomical Union (IAU).

Two more moons of Uranus have recently been sighted. They will be listed as Uranus XVI and Uranus XVII until the IAU General Assembly meets to review the findings, in August 2000. At that time, official names will be assigned. The astronomers who discovered these moons have suggested the names Caliban and Sycorax, two characters from William Shakespeare's play *The Tempest*. (Uranus's other moons are also named after characters in plays by Shakespeare.)

• OUR MYSTERIOUS MOON •

The Earth and Moon are unique in the solar system. Even though many planets have moons, few are as large compared to their planet as ours. Some astronomers believe we should call the Earth and Moon a "double planet" instead of a planet with a single moon. No one knows why our moon is so large or how it was created. There are several different theories, but each one presents unsolved mysteries.

1. The Earth and Moon formed at the same time. When all the planets were forming, the Earth and Moon grew around each other.
Unsolved mystery: If the Earth and Moon formed at the same time, they should be made of the same materials, but they aren't.

THE EARTH AND THE MOON: WERE THEY FORMED TOGETHER? ▼

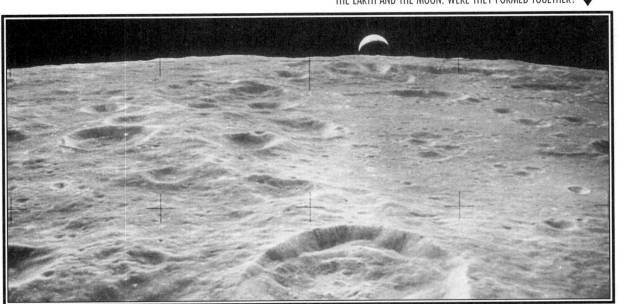

2. The Earth and Moon were originally one body. The Earth and Moon used to be one planet, but as the Earth cooled it bulged and ejected some material into space, which formed the Moon.

Unsolved mystery: Earth's gravity is strong enough to have pulled all this loose debris back down to the planet surface.

3. The Moon was created by a gigantic meteor. Early in its life, Earth was struck by a large meteor, sending a large amount of debris into space, which formed the Moon.

Unsolved mystery: The Moon is as old as, and maybe even older than, the Earth. There isn't enough time for this to have happened.

4. The Moon was captured by the Earth. The Moon formed elsewhere, maybe even outside the solar system, and then was "captured" by Earth's gravity.

Unsolved mystery: The Earth is too small to have captured such a large body.

For further information and images of the Moon, visit:
http://nssdc.gsfc.nasa.gov/planetary/planets/moonpage.html

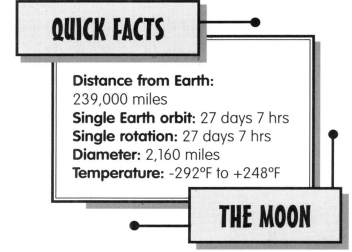

QUICK FACTS

THE MOON

Distance from Earth:
239,000 miles
Single Earth orbit: 27 days 7 hrs
Single rotation: 27 days 7 hrs
Diameter: 2,160 miles
Temperature: -292°F to +248°F

• THE FAR SIDE OF THE MOON •

Because the lunar day exactly matches the time the Moon takes to orbit the Earth, we always see the same face of the Moon. For many centuries, astronomers wondered what the far side looked like. In October 1959, when the Soviet (Russian) space probe *Luna 3* became the first craft to orbit the Moon, the mystery was solved.

Luna 3's images of the far side revealed a landscape riddled with impact craters. (The Earth shields the near side of the Moon from many incoming meteors, but the far side is exposed to bombardment from space.) The far side of the Moon also has more mountains and fewer molten "seas" than the side that faces us. (These "seas" are not really seas but smooth plains of rock left over from ancient lava flows.) To see images from the far side of the Moon, visit: http://www.hawastsoc.org/solar/cap/moon/farside.htm

• MORE MOON MYSTERIES •

Along with the question of how our Moon came into existence are other lunar mysteries that space scientists have never been able to explain.

1. The Moon's age. The Moon may be older than the Earth (which would be impossible if they were formed at the same time). Some of the rocks brought back by the Apollo missions appear to be between 4.3 and 5.3 billion years old—but the oldest known rocks on Earth are only 3.7 billion years old! Even stranger, the *regolith* the rocks were found in is as much as a billion years older.

2. Rust-proof Iron. Iron particles brought back from the Moon have never rusted, even after several years on Earth. Rust-proof iron is unknown in the universe, and scientists are at a loss to explain how it could exist.

3. Lunar water. The Moon is generally considered to be drier than a desert, without even a trace of water inside its dusty rocks. Yet space scientists were stunned to find large clouds of water vapor, 100 miles wide, blowing across the lunar surface.

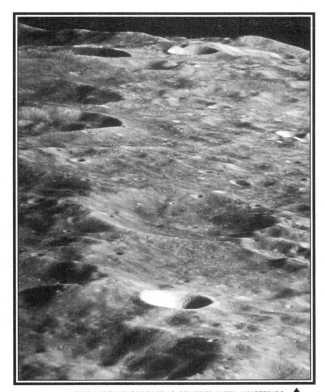

THE MOON'S SURFACE IS COVERED WITH MYSTERIES ▲

4. Lunar glass. Some of the lunar surface is covered with glass, of a type created by intense heat, such as that from atomic explosions or lightning strikes, instead of meteor impacts. The Moon would have to have been subjected to heat it would not have encountered (had it formed alongside the Earth some billions of years ago) in order for this "lunar glass" to have been created.

SPACE JARGON

Regolith: Lunar soil, made of dust, crushed rock, and other fine particles.

Cosmic Mysteries

Space has always been an amazing, magical, and mysterious place. In ancient times, the twinkling stars were a mystery. A hundred years ago, so were the other planets. Today, we know much more about the stars and planets, but many more mysteries yet remain to be solved.

• IS THE UNIVERSE INFINITE? •

One of the great remaining mysteries is the size of the universe. Is it expanding? Does it go on forever? How big is it? Astronomers believe the universe began as a single point some fifteen billion years ago. But if it's not infinite, what does that mean? Could you travel to the edge of the universe and be stopped by some invisible barrier? Nobody knows for sure.

• THE MYSTERY OF THE MISSING NEUTRINOS •

One of the most baffling mysteries confronting scientists is the matter of the "missing" neutrinos. Neutrinos are produced in huge numbers by the fusion reactions that power the Sun. They are some of the most abundant particles in the universe, and trillions of them stream toward Earth every second. But neutrinos are so small that gravity has almost no effect on them, so they pass straight through Earth—and us—without ever being noticed.

Scientists have devised a way to detect neutrinos passing through Earth by placing huge vats of chlorine deep underground. (Chlorine is a chemical that reacts when struck by neutrino particles.) Astronomers predicted that they would detect twenty-five neutrinos striking the vats each month, but thus far monthly tests have detected only eight neutrinos. Where are all the missing neutrinos? For more information on the search for neutrinos, visit: http://neutrino.pc.helsinki.fi/neutrino/index.html

• THE MYSTERY OF DARK MATTER •

One of the most perplexing mysteries facing scientists is how much mass the universe contains. Using telescopes to count galaxies and estimate total mass, astronomers are able to account for only 1 percent of the mass that should have been created in the Big Bang, according to current theory.

As much as 99 percent of our universe may be made of "dark matter," a mysterious substance undetected by astronomers but existing throughout the cosmos. Dark matter is not really dark, like charcoal or some other kind of dust. (If it were, astronomers could see it as it blotted out stars, the same way the Moon blots out the Sun during a lunar eclipse.) It is simply material that doesn't reflect light or emit radiation—in other words, matter that cannot be detected with existing technology.

In June 1998, scientists discovered that the neutrino, an "invisible" particle once believed to have no mass at all, actually has a fraction of the mass of an electron. (Other than the neutrino, the electron is the lightest known particle.) Since the universe is literally filled with neutrinos, their combined mass may be enough to account for the missing dark matter.

Determining how much mass the universe has is the key to understanding the future. Too little mass means the universe will continue expanding forever, growing ever colder. A certain amount of mass will stop the universe's expansion, leaving everything "frozen" in space. More mass will cause our universe's expansion to slow and then reverse the pull of gravity until everything collapses back into itself in a "Big Crunch" (which may give birth to a new Big Bang and begin the cycle all over again).

• A MYSTERIOUS ATTRACTION •

Astronomers have discovered that entire galaxies are being pulled across space toward some powerful, unknown source. In fact, an entire group of galaxies appears to be headed in the direction of what the sky charts call the Southern Cross, pulled along at millions of miles per hour.

How many stars are rushing toward this spot in space? Our Milky Way Galaxy alone contains 100 billion stars, yet it's only a small dot on the edge of a larger constellation of galaxies called the Virgo Supercluster. And both the Virgo Supercluster and the Hydra-Centaurus Supercluster, made up of many trillions of stars, are being pulled toward this mysterious attractor in space.

• THE MYSTERY OF ANTIMATTER •

Few mysteries of space are as exciting to think about or as important to our survival as the question of antimatter.

Antimatter was first discussed in 1928 by physicist Paul Dirac. Dirac calculated that every particle that makes up our universe—the protons, neutrons, and electrons that exist inside atoms—has an equal and opposite particle, an antiparticle. If matter and antimatter meet, each destroys the other instantaneously in a cataclysmic explosion.

In 1932, scientists proved that antimatter really exists. Today, researchers produce microscopic amounts of antimatter in laboratories all over the world, but it is always destroyed by contact with matter immediately after coming into existence. Why hasn't the entire universe been destroyed as matter and antimatter explode all around us? No one knows for sure. Perhaps antimatter exists in space but not in our galaxy. Perhaps we live in a universe of matter and have not yet met an antimatter universe. The National Aeronautics and Space Administration (NASA) plans to launch an antimatter collector into space to see how much antimatter is out there. If antimatter is widespread, then so is the possibility of our own destruction.

• THE MYSTERY OF GRAVITONS •

Astrophysicists have long wondered how gravity exists in the vacuum of space. What force sends signals across the vast, empty distances? They theorize that gravity may move in invisible waves of particles called *gravitons*, each carrying invisible messages between objects in space.

Scientists have not yet been able to detect gravitons, but they are building complicated gravity-wave detectors that they hope will provide answers about this most basic of forces.

• THE MYSTERY OF TIME •

Everybody dreams of traveling through time. And everybody knows time moves forward, one day after another. Still, according to the laws of physics, nothing prevents time from going backward.

If the universe were collapsing instead of expanding, time might move in reverse. The same might be true if the planets orbited the Sun in the opposite direction. But there is nothing in space mechanics that says these things can't happen. At a subatomic level, particles can move in either direction.

In theory, if all the particles happened to move in the right direction, we could see reversals of time all around us. A leaf could rise up off the ground and reattach itself to a tree. Spilled milk could collect together and flow back into a glass. So why don't these things happen? Probably because so many particles make up our everyday world. A single particle may move in one direction or another, but as a whole the march of time moves only in one direction.

• BLACK HOLES •

Black holes are among the most powerful and mysterious objects in the universe. Are they portals through time and space? Are they tunnels between our universe and other, unknown universes? Are they gigantic destroyers of stars and planets, or a place where space particles are born? No one knows for certain.

What is known is that black holes are formed from dead stars. When a large star has burned up all its fuel, it can no longer radiate heat and light outward and instead grows dark. Sometimes, the star collapses inward with so much force that its gravity allows nothing to escape—not even rays of light. That is why black holes are too dark to be seen.

If we can't see black holes, how can we know they exist? We can watch what happens to the space around a black hole, called the *event horizon*, where interstellar gas, planets,

SPACE JARGON

Event horizon: The outer edge of a black hole, the last point at which astronomers can detect light rays, interstellar gases, and other deep-space matter.

STARS AND OTHER GASES ARE PULLED INTO A BLACK HOLE'S POWERFUL GRAVITY ▶

and even entire solar systems are pulled by the gravitational field and vanish from view.

Black holes may exist throughout the entire universe. Astronomers have even detected a large black hole at the core of our own galaxy, equal in size to 2.6 million Suns, and drawing stars inward at the rate of 600 miles per second! For more information on black holes, visit: http://cossc.gsfc.nasa.gov/gamma/new_win/nw10.html

SPACE PIONEERS

Stephen Hawking (1942–) is living proof that people can travel the universe without ever leaving their seats. Hawking's seat is a wheelchair, since he suffers from lateral sclerosis (Lou Gehrig's Disease), which leaves him unable to move or speak. The disease hasn't stopped Hawking from becoming one of history's greatest space physicists—and the world's leading expert on black holes. In fact, he holds the same position at England's Cambridge University that Sir Isaac Newton once held.

How does Hawking communicate his ideas about time and space? He has a special keyboard at his fingertips, and uses just two fingers to tap out a message letter by letter. A computer then translates his writing into artificial speech, which is spoken by a computer voice.

STEPHEN HAWKING

• IS TIME TRAVEL POSSIBLE? •

Scientists have often wondered what happens to things that get pulled into a black hole. Are they burned up like fuel inside a gigantic furnace? Or are black holes more like tunnels, connecting our known universe with countless other universes?

At a black hole's event horizon, space and time are believed to be distorted, making travel over great distances possible (at least in theory). This space-time connector is often called a wormhole. Matter falling into a black hole might pass through a wormhole and enter another universe from the black hole's opposite end, a "white hole."

Do we have white holes in our own universe? Some astronomers have theorized that quasars, which release huge amounts of energy from unknown sources, might be white holes. But for now, no one can be sure whether white holes, or wormholes, truly exist. Perhaps all wormholes, if they exist, link our universe with other universes. Albert Einstein theorized that wormholes might be interstellar passageways connecting different parts of our own universe together like intergalactic expressways through space and time.

• DOES EXTRATERRESTRIAL LIFE EXIST? •

Astronomers generally believe that life exists throughout the universe, but so far none has been discovered beyond Earth. In 1976, NASA sent two *Viking* spacecraft to Mars, where a robot arm scooped up some soil to search for microorganisms. These days, NASA is looking even farther away: Missions are planned to send probes to Jupiter and Saturn. We may see our first glimpse of extraterrestrial life as soon as the beginning of the next century.

• A FORMULA FOR LIFE IN THE UNIVERSE •

Even though we have not yet found life beyond the Earth, astronomer Frank Drake has devised a formula to estimate the odds that it exists throughout the universe:

multiply the number of stars in the Milky Way Galaxy
by the number of stars that have planets
by the number of planets that can support life
by the number of planets where life actually arises
by the number of planets where intelligent life develops
by the number of planets where technology develops
by the span of time a technological civilization survives

Let's apply this formula to the Milky Way Galaxy to estimate how many advanced, technological civilizations like our own might exist: There are hundreds of billions of stars in the Milky Way . . . Each shines for billions of years . . . Most of these stars may have planets . . . even if only a couple of planets surrounding each star are suitable for life and only 1 percent of those planets develop intelligent, technological civilizations, we would live in a galaxy with many millions of worlds like our own. And our galaxy is only one of many billions throughout the universe!

• AN INTERGALACTIC PHONE CALL •

As long as humans have looked at the stars, we have wondered: "Is anybody out there? Are we alone in the universe?" As yet, no one can say for certain. But the Jet Propulsion Laboratory (JPL) is using radio telescopes to create a detailed map of the entire sky in a project called the High Resolution Microwave Survey (HRMS).

Part of the project, called the Search for Extraterrestrial Intelligence (SETI), involves searching for signals that might be sent by intelligent life elsewhere in the universe. Radio waves are very powerful and travel great distances through the universe, much farther than the visible light of glowing stars. Even if no alien civilization has sent a message in our direction, we may still detect its radio signals. Every radio and television signal ever sent over the airwaves on Earth has escaped into space and could be detected by intelligent life on other planets using similar technology.

What if extraterrestrial signals are detected? JPL plans to relay the information to other astronomers for confirmation and then release the findings to the public. The day may come when we are certain that there are other creatures living elsewhere in the universe. For more information on the SETI project, visit: http://www.seti-inst.edu

• FOSSILS OF ALIEN LIFE •

While SETI scientists scan the skies with large radio telescopes, searching for signals that might prove the existence of extraterrestrial intelligence, other researchers are searching for evidence of alien life right here on Earth.

The Earth is constantly bombarded by small meteorites, many of which can be found in remote regions such as Australia and Antarctica. Two meteorites discovered thus far may contain fossils of ancient alien bacteria living at the time the meteorites were formed.

One fossil-bearing meteorite come from Mars. (Scientists can tell a meteorite's origin from each planet's unique chemistry.) The second fossil was found in the Murchison meteorite, which was discovered in Australia. Astronomers are uncertain where this meteorite originated, but it appears to have fallen to Earth from beyond the Earth-Moon-Mars region.

Both meteorites have been x-rayed and scanned with electron microscopes in order to reveal their inner structure in detail. These simple fossils may indeed be the first proof we have that life exists elsewhere in the universe, but more research is required to confirm the findings. For more information on Martian meteorites, visit: http://www.jpl.nasa.gov/snc

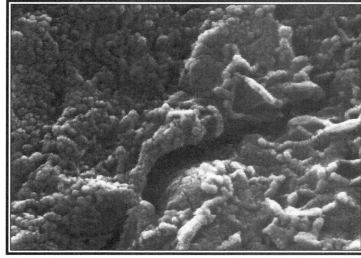

DOES THIS MARTIAN METEORITE HOLD FOSSILS OF EXTRATERRESTRIAL LIFE?

48

• LIFE IN THE CLOUDS •

It is easy to forget that life elsewhere in the universe doesn't have to look like life on Earth. Planets very different from our own could develop creatures specially adapted to their world. Astronomers Carl Sagan and E. E. Salpeter once proposed that life could even exist on a gas giant like Jupiter.

Jupiter is a planet made up of gases—mostly hydrogen, helium, methane, water, and ammonia. It doesn't really have a surface to stand on. (It does have a solid core, but the heat and pressure are probably too severe for life to exist there.) Jupiter is like a giant cloud planet, and for creatures to exist there they would have to live in the clouds their entire life.

On Earth, we know that hot air balloons (which are filled with hydrogen or helium) can float in the clouds. What if Jupiter had giant hydrogen-filled creatures, floating like hot air balloons? They could move themselves about the planet by shooting out gusts of gas, sinking lower and rising high in the clouds again. Sagan called such creatures "floaters," and nothing we know about the universe today says they couldn't exist!

SPACE TALK

"I would be very ashamed of my civilization if we did not try to find out if there is life in outer space."
—Carl Sagan, astronomer and author

• ALIEN ASTRONAUTS IN AFRICA? •

Have alien astronauts visited Earth in the past and met with ancient humans? One space mystery, involving a West African tribe called the Dogon, suggests this may be so.

The Dogon who live today are descended from people who lived in Egypt, North Africa, many centuries ago. They have a long history that has been passed down from generation to generation through storytelling. In the 1940s, two French scientists, Marcel Griaule and Germaine Dieterlen, visited the Dogon people to hear some of these ancient stories. The Dogon told them that the star Sirius, 8.6 light-years from Earth, has an invisible companion star that is smaller but heavier than Sirius itself. The Dogon also explained that this companion orbits Sirius once every 50 years.

Many years later, in 1970, astronomers discovered that Sirius did have a white-dwarf companion star, smaller and heavier than Sirius itself—with a fifty-year orbit. Everything the Dogon had said was true! But how could they have known about Sirius's companion (called Sirius B) in the 1940s, even if they had access to the telescope or astronomy books of that time? The story of Sirius B had been told in Dogon mythology for many centuries.

Some people believe this story proves that the Dogon people were visited by extraterrestrials at some time far in the past and were told about Sirius B at that time.

THE SPACE AGE BEGINS

As long as people have looked to the heavens, they have dreamed of traveling in space. What began as pure fantasy soon became the stuff of science fiction stories that thrilled readers all over the world. In this century, generations of scientists have developed sophisticated new technologies to make the **Space Age** a reality at last.

• FIRST STEPS •

History's long march toward space began with some very notable successes:

A.D. 62   Heron, a Greek inventor, demonstrates thrust—an essential property of light—with a sphere spun by steam forced from nozzles.

850   The Chinese invent gunpowder fireworks.

1232   The Chinese use "flaming" rockets to repel Mongol invaders, combining gunpowder with flight.

1680   Peter the Great creates the Rocket Works, a factory to manufacture rockets for the Russian Army.

1780   Prince Hyder Ali of India uses iron rockets against Britain, achieving distances of up to five miles.

1813   William Moore publishes *A Treatise on the Motion of Rockets*, specifying the mathematical requirements of rocket flight.

1840   William Hale adds fins to rockets, stabilizing flight and improving trajectory control.

1865   Author Jules Verne writes *From the Earth to the Moon*, a story about a manned capsule launched to the Moon.

SPACE PIONEERS

Jules Verne (1828–1905) loved adventure. As a child, he ran away from home to become a cabin boy on a merchant ship. He began to write adventure stories about exploring new frontiers, such as *Five Weeks in a Balloon, A Journey to the Center of the Earth*, and *20,000 Leagues Under the Sea*. Verne also wrote a space book called *From the Earth to the Moon*, about a capsule launched into space to land on the Moon. In the story, he described the force of takeoff, the heat generated by Earth's atmosphere, the weightlessness of space, and many other aspects of space travel—all with amazing accuracy more than a hundred years before such a feat became reality.

The book caused a worldwide sensation, and inspired generations of schoolchildren to study science. These same children would grow up to launch the Space Age, making Verne's story a reality.

JULES VERNE

JULES VERNE'S *FROM THE EARTH TO THE MOON* ▲

• NEW FUEL FOR THE STARS •

As a young boy, Robert H. Goddard was captivated by H. G. Wells's science fiction story *War of the Worlds*, about an invasion of Earth by space-faring Martians. While in school, he began to design rockets, publishing his findings in a paper entitled *A Method of Reaching Extreme Altitudes*. When people laughed at his ideas of sending a rocket to the Moon, Goddard withdrew and decided to keep his ideas to himself.

Goddard realized that rockets could be powered by liquid fuels instead of solid materials such as gunpowder. A few years later, from his aunt's farm, he launched the world's first liquid-fueled rocket—powered by a combination of liquid oxygen and hydrogen. On its first flight, the rocket rose only forty-one feet off the ground. Within a short while, however, Goddard's rockets were streaming thousands of feet into the air.

Today, most rockets use liquid fuels, and Goddard is widely hailed as "the father of American rocketry." To commemorate his contributions to the Space Age, NASA's Goddard Flight Center is named in his honor.

SPACE PIONEERS

As a child, Konstantin Tsiolkovsky (1857–1935) nearly went deaf as the result of scarlet fever. He stayed home from school, reading and studying mathematics. Tsiolkovsky was very excited by Jules Verne's story about launching a spaceship to the Moon. He began to design spaceships and rockets of his own and wrote science fiction stories about satellites, space colonies, and astronauts in orbit. Because most of Tsiolkovsky's ideas seemed so impossible, few people paid attention to his work. But this quiet Russian genius calculated exactly what was required to send a rocket into space. He was, in a sense, the father of the Space Age.

Although Tsiolkovsky never built a rocket himself, his work inspired many others who did. To honor his contributions to space exploration, a crater on the Moon is named for Tsiolkovsky.

KONSTANTIN TSIOLKOVSKY

• SEEING "WAYS TO SPACEFLIGHT" •

While Goddard designed rockets in America and Tsiolkovsky did the same in Russia, a third rocket pioneer—physicist Hermann Oberth—was publishing his ideas about rocketry in Germany. Like his counterparts, Oberth wrote research papers detailing the mechanics of space flight and built rockets to demonstrate his theories. Oberth's popular book *Ways to Spaceflight* proposed orbiting space stations where rockets might refuel, and pondered the effects of weightlessness on humans in space.

More than anything else, Oberth made people believe that the Space Age had begun for real and that space travel had become more than just a fantasy in a science fiction book.

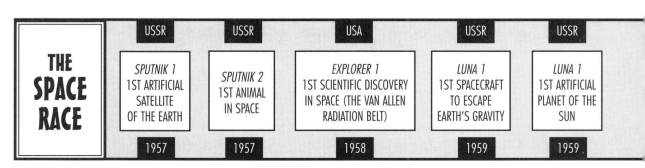

THE SPACE RACE	USSR	USSR	USA	USSR	USSR
	SPUTNIK 1 1ST ARTIFICIAL SATELLITE OF THE EARTH	SPUTNIK 2 1ST ANIMAL IN SPACE	EXPLORER 1 1ST SCIENTIFIC DISCOVERY IN SPACE (THE VAN ALLEN RADIATION BELT)	LUNA 1 1ST SPACECRAFT TO ESCAPE EARTH'S GRAVITY	LUNA 1 1ST ARTIFICIAL PLANET OF THE SUN
	1957	1957	1958	1959	1959

• THE SPACE RACE •

The Space Race officially began in 1957, when the Soviet Union (USSR, now Russia) launched a small, round orb called *Sputnik* into Earth orbit. It was our planet's first artificial (man-made) satellite. Americans heard the sound of *Sputnik* beeping on their radios as it passed overhead and worried about falling behind the Russians in exploring the frontier of space. The Space Race was on, and each country tried to top the other with new and exciting achievements.

Today, exploring space is no longer a competition. Many nations work together in friendship and cooperation, and everything learned is freely shared. The future of space exploration will be a global achievement for all people.

• THE FIRST SPACEWALK •

The first human to "walk in space" (float) was Soviet cosmonaut Alexei Leonov. On March 18, 1965, aboard the Soviet capsule *Voskhod 2*, Leonov put on a space suit and climbed into *Voskhod*'s airlock, sealing off the interior hatchway. The cosmonaut then opened the exterior hatchway and eased himself out into space, attached to his spaceship by nothing more than a slim safety line.

Leonov knew that if he were to break loose, there would be no way to return to his capsule—he would float away into the vast emptiness of space. But after twelve exciting minutes of floating freely, he climbed back safely inside his orbiting "lifeboat."

• "COME BACK INSIDE NOW!" •

The first American to walk in space was astronaut Ed White, orbiting the Earth aboard *Gemini 4* on June 3, 1965. NASA controllers planned for White to take a twelve-minute "walk" outside the capsule, connected to the spacecraft by a thirty-foot tether.

White enjoyed the experience so much, however, that he refused to return to *Gemini*.

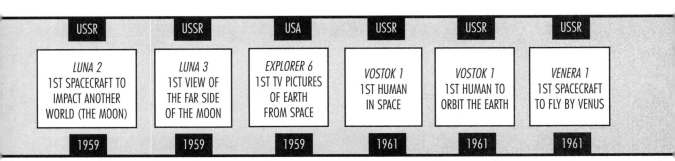

USSR	USSR	USA	USSR	USSR	USSR
LUNA 2 1ST SPACECRAFT TO IMPACT ANOTHER WORLD (THE MOON)	*LUNA 3* 1ST VIEW OF THE FAR SIDE OF THE MOON	*EXPLORER 6* 1ST TV PICTURES OF EARTH FROM SPACE	*VOSTOK 1* 1ST HUMAN IN SPACE	*VOSTOK 1* 1ST HUMAN TO ORBIT THE EARTH	*VENERA 1* 1ST SPACECRAFT TO FLY BY VENUS
1959	1959	1959	1961	1961	1961

"I'm not coming in . . . this is fun," he exclaimed. Ground controllers reminded White that he was moving at 17,500 miles per hour. Within four minutes he would cross over to the dark side of the Earth, where the sudden cold (-250°F in Earth's shadow) could be deadly. White's companion in the *Gemini 4* capsule, astronaut Jim McDivitt, ordered the spacewalker back inside: "Get back in here before it gets dark."

White climbed back inside just twenty seconds before the capsule crossed into night. He had space walked for twenty-one minutes—almost twice as long as originally planned!

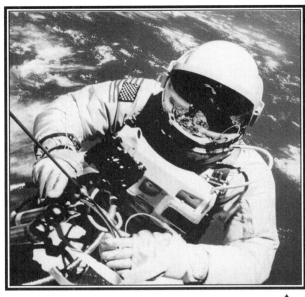

ED WHITE, FIRST AMERICAN ASTRONAUT TO WALK IN SPACE ▲

• ANIMALNAUTS •

Humans aren't the only earthlings who've gone into space. Since the earliest days of rocketry, animals have been sent aloft in hopes of teaching scientists about the conditions above Earth's atmosphere. These brave "animalnauts" have served as the world's first space pioneers.

After the successful launch of the unmanned *Sputnik 1* satellite, the Russians were eager to send living creatures into space. *Sputnik 2*, launched in 1957, carried a small dog named Laika ("Barker" in English). Unfortunately, no plans were made to return Laika to Earth, and the capsule's life-support systems kept her alive for only a few days. Forty years later, Laika was memorialized with a special plaque at the Russian research center where she trained for her historic mission.

In 1959–61, the United States launched a series of *Mercury* capsules on suborbital flights. These spacecraft carried chimpanzees named Sam, Miss Sam, and Ham in place of astronauts. All three chimpanzees returned safely to Earth. The first orbital flight was launched in November 1961, carrying a chimp named Enos.

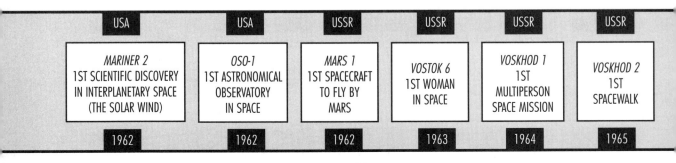

USA	USA	USSR	USSR	USSR	USSR
MARINER 2 1ST SCIENTIFIC DISCOVERY IN INTERPLANETARY SPACE (THE SOLAR WIND)	OSO-1 1ST ASTRONOMICAL OBSERVATORY IN SPACE	MARS 1 1ST SPACECRAFT TO FLY BY MARS	VOSTOK 6 1ST WOMAN IN SPACE	VOSKHOD 1 1ST MULTIPERSON SPACE MISSION	VOSKHOD 2 1ST SPACEWALK
1962	1962	1962	1963	1964	1965

Throughout the years, many other creatures have traveled into space—including rats, newts, frogs, bees, flies, shrimp, and fish (even jellyfish!).

At least two animals may continue to travel in space in the future, but not as the subjects of experiments. One day, astronauts will probably bring dogs and cats along on long space voyages between worlds simply for companionship. For more information on animal astronauts, visit: http://ham.spa.umn.edu/kris/animals.html

Spinning in space. Space scientists have always been interested in the effects of weightlessness—not just on astronauts, but on all living things. In 1973, Skylab astronauts carried along two very special passengers named Arabella and Anita. Their mission was to weave in space. Arabella and Anita weren't seamstresses . . . they were spiders!

Arabella was allowed to spin as soon as she arrived in orbit. Due to the effects of zero gravity, her first few webs were tangled, but after a couple of days she spun normally again. Anita, who was kept from spinning for a couple of days until she had adjusted to weightlessness, spun her first web as perfectly as on Earth.

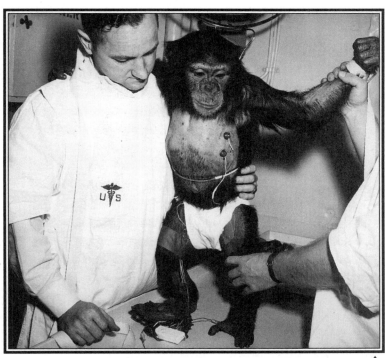

AMERICA'S FIRST ASTRONAUT WAS A CHIMPANZEE NAMED SAM ▲

USSR	USSR	USSR	USA	USA
VENERA 3 1ST SPACECRAFT IN ATMOSPHERE OF ANOTHER PLANET (VENUS)	LUNA 10 1ST SPACECRAFT TO ORBIT ANOTHER WORLD (THE MOON)	LUNA 9 1ST SUCCESSFUL LANDING ON ANOTHER WORLD (THE MOON)	APOLLO 8 1ST MANNED ORBIT OF ANOTHER WORLD (THE MOON)	APOLLO 11 1ST HUMAN LANDING ON ANOTHER WORLD (THE MOON)
1966	1966	1966	1968	1969

• LANDING ON THE MOON •

Few adventures have thrilled or challenged humankind as much as landing astronauts on the Moon. The Moon, Earth's only natural satellite, orbits so close to Earth that it looms large and bright in the sky. The Moon has little atmosphere, and little of practical value to offer. It is a dusty, barren world, covered by craters and the wide, smooth plains of ancient lava flows. Yet it is our Moon, and it beckons us. Exploring the Moon is like visiting a part of our own world.

In 1958, the United States and the Soviet Union (Russia) embarked on a frantic race to reach the Moon. Both countries risked lives and spent huge amounts of money trying to outdo each other's achievements. Yet from this effort the Space Age was born, and

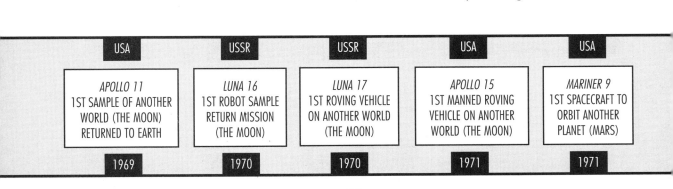

USA	USSR	USSR	USA	USA
APOLLO 11 1ST SAMPLE OF ANOTHER WORLD (THE MOON) RETURNED TO EARTH	LUNA 16 1ST ROBOT SAMPLE RETURN MISSION (THE MOON)	LUNA 17 1ST ROVING VEHICLE ON ANOTHER WORLD (THE MOON)	APOLLO 15 1ST MANNED ROVING VEHICLE ON ANOTHER WORLD (THE MOON)	MARINER 9 1ST SPACECRAFT TO ORBIT ANOTHER PLANET (MARS)
1969	1970	1970	1971	1971

technologies were developed that have served us ever since. We owe a lot to having been a little "*lunatic.*"

On July 21, 1969, when astronauts Neil Armstrong and Edwin "Buzz" Aldrin stepped onto the lunar surface, the great race was over at last. The two men set out an American flag, set up scientific experiments, and collected rock samples. But Armstrong and Aldrin had flown to the Moon representing all Earth's nations and peoples. They carried goodwill speeches from twenty-three world leaders and left behind a lunar plaque which read:

Here Men From Planet Earth First Set Foot Upon the Moon
July 1969 A.D.
We Came In Peace For All Mankind

WORD ORIGINS

Lunatic: The word lunatic comes from the Latin word *luna*, meaning "moon." The word literally means "moonstruck"; ancient people believed that the Moon had such a powerful effect on people that it could drive them insane.

SPACE TALK

"Here's one small step for a man . . . one giant leap for mankind."
—Neil Armstrong,
first human to walk on the Moon,
stepping off *Apollo 11* lander
onto the lunar surface

USA	USA	USSR	USA	USA	USA
PIONEER 10 1ST SPACECRAFT TO FLY BY JUPITER	MARINER 10 1ST TWO-PLANET MISSION (VENUS & MERCURY)	VENERA 9/10 1ST PHOTOS OF VENUSIAN SURFACE	VIKING 1 1ST SUCCESSFUL MARS LANDING	VIKING 1 1ST SPACECRAFT TO SEARCH FOR LIFE ON ANOTHER PLANET (MARS)	PIONEER 11 1ST SPACECRAFT TO FLY BY SATURN
1973	1974	1975	1976	1976	1977

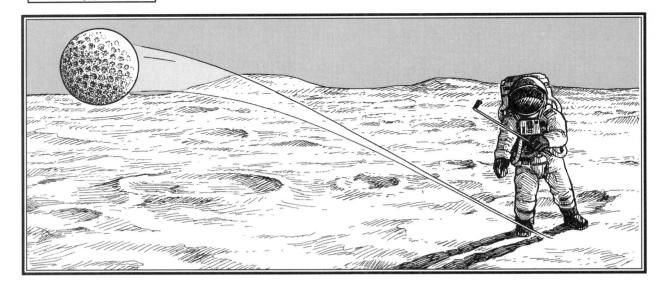

• PAR FOR THE MOON •

In 1961, Alan B. Shepard became America's first astronaut, completing a suborbital flight in a *Mercury* capsule. Ten years later, Shepard realized his greatest dream—traveling to the Moon as commander of the *Apollo 14* mission.

What did Shepard do to commemorate his historic achievement? After completing his official duties, he took a golf ball from his pocket and dropped it on the lunar surface. Using a makeshift golf club, he swung at the ball but miss-hit, sending it only a short distance. Shepard dropped another ball on the soft lunar soil and tried again. This time, he announced, the ball flew "for miles and miles" in the thin lunar gravity. It was the first time golf had been played on another world!

• THE MOON TREES •

Everybody knows the Apollo astronauts returned to Earth with samples of lunar rocks and soil. The *Apollo 14* crew, however, returned home with something more: hundreds of

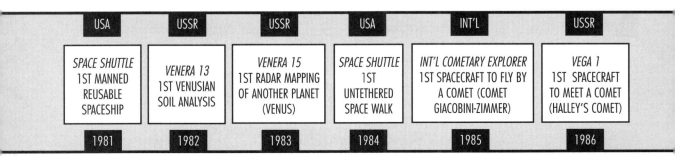

USA	USSR	USSR	USA	INT'L	USSR
SPACE SHUTTLE 1ST MANNED REUSABLE SPACESHIP	VENERA 13 1ST VENUSIAN SOIL ANALYSIS	VENERA 15 1ST RADAR MAPPING OF ANOTHER PLANET (VENUS)	SPACE SHUTTLE 1ST UNTETHERED SPACE WALK	INT'L COMETARY EXPLORER 1ST SPACECRAFT TO FLY BY A COMET (COMET GIACOBINI-ZIMMER)	VEGA 1 1ST SPACECRAFT TO MEET A COMET (HALLEY'S COMET)
1981	1982	1983	1984	1985	1986

trees! How? Trees can't grow in the Moon's airless, waterless environment, of course, but astronaut Stuart Roosa carried hundreds of tree seeds with him on his lunar voyage.

Before becoming an astronaut, Roosa had been a "smoke jumper," a fire fighter who parachutes into forest fires to save trees from burning. When he was selected for the *Apollo 14* mission, NASA agreed to send some seeds into space to see whether they would grow after being returned to Earth. Seeds from five different kinds of trees were selected for the mission: Douglas fir, loblolly pine, redwood, sweet gum, and sycamore.

After *Apollo 14*'s return, the seeds were given to many different states. Nearly all grew into healthy trees, seemingly unaffected by their half-million-mile journey. One tree was planted at the White House, another at NASA headquarters, and others as far away as Brazil, Japan, and Switzerland. These are the "Moon trees," a living reminder of the men who first traveled to another world. A list of Moon tree locations can be found at: http://nssdc.gsfc.nasa.gov/planetary/lunar/moon_tree.html

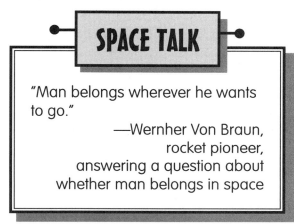

SPACE TALK

"Man belongs wherever he wants to go."

—Wernher Von Braun, rocket pioneer, answering a question about whether man belongs in space

• THE DANGERS OF SPACE TRAVEL •

What's the most dangerous part of a space mission? The launch? Achieving orbit? Reentering Earth's atmosphere? Surprisingly, the greatest risk to NASA's space vehicles is the road trip needed to move them from the Vertical Assembly Building to the launchpad! Everyday bumps and vibrations along the road can build up tremendous stress in a rocket, creating structural weaknesses that could endanger an entire mission.

NASA has constructed special vehicles called "crawler-transporters" to transfer their rockets while keeping them in an upright position. During the Apollo missions, each space

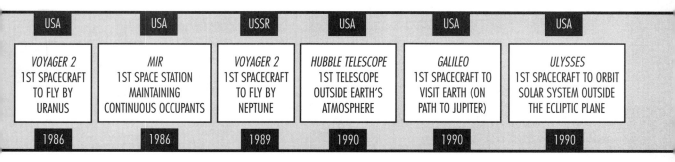

USA	USA	USSR	USA	USA	USA
VOYAGER 2 1ST SPACECRAFT TO FLY BY URANUS	MIR 1ST SPACE STATION MAINTAINING CONTINUOUS OCCUPANTS	VOYAGER 2 1ST SPACECRAFT TO FLY BY NEPTUNE	HUBBLE TELESCOPE 1ST TELESCOPE OUTSIDE EARTH'S ATMOSPHERE	GALILEO 1ST SPACECRAFT TO VISIT EARTH (ON PATH TO JUPITER)	ULYSSES 1ST SPACECRAFT TO ORBIT SOLAR SYSTEM OUTSIDE THE ECLIPTIC PLANE
1986	1986	1989	1990	1990	1990

vehicle traveled the three and a half miles from hangar to launchpad in eight hours—moving at a top speed of only one mile per hour!

• SPACE DISASTERS •

Space is a dangerous place to be, but so is Earth when you work with gigantic liquid-fueled rockets that can explode unexpectedly with tremendous force.

Since the Space Age began, at least 243 people have been killed while training for or participating in space missions. Each tragedy has resulted in a temporary shutdown of the space program to allow time to analyze and solve the problems that led to the mishap. Each disaster has taught scientists how to make space a safer place in which to live and work.

THE MOST DANGEROUS PART OF A SPACE MISSION: ▲ TRANSPORTING THE ROCKET TO THE LAUNCHPAD!

• THE FIRST BIG DISASTER •

The earliest days of space exploration were among the most dangerous, since every piece of equipment and every procedure was being tested for the first time.

The worst space disaster in history occurred on October 24, 1960, when a gigantic rocket at the Soviet Union's Baikonur Cosmodrome exploded on the launchpad, killing 165 workers. The cause of the accident turned out to be "human error": Technicians had forgotten to close fuel valves connecting the first and second stages of the rocket, resulting in a leak and an explosion during ignition.

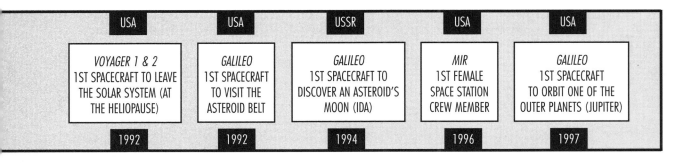

USA	USA	USSR	USA	USA
VOYAGER 1 & 2 1ST SPACECRAFT TO LEAVE THE SOLAR SYSTEM (AT THE HELIOPAUSE)	GALILEO 1ST SPACECRAFT TO VISIT THE ASTEROID BELT	GALILEO 1ST SPACECRAFT TO DISCOVER AN ASTEROID'S MOON (IDA)	MIR 1ST FEMALE SPACE STATION CREW MEMBER	GALILEO 1ST SPACECRAFT TO ORBIT ONE OF THE OUTER PLANETS (JUPITER)
1992	1992	1994	1996	1997

• THE *APOLLO 1* LAUNCHPAD FIRE •

The United States experienced a launchpad tragedy of its own on January 27, 1967, when a sudden flash fire engulfed the *Apollo 1* capsule during a launch countdown rehearsal. As they sat strapped in the cockpit, astronauts Virgil I. "Gus" Grissom, Edward H. White, Jr., and Roger B. Chaffee were excited about inaugurating a new era in space. The Apollo series was the beginning of America's Moon missions. During a routine countdown rehearsal exercise, however, a faulty wire sparked in the flammable, oxygen-rich capsule, igniting a flash fire that quickly surrounded the men trapped inside.

The burning astronauts tried to open their capsule door from inside, but the *Apollo 1* capsule had not been equipped with explosive bolts that might have allowed the maintenance crew to blow open the door from outside. By the time the crew finally opened the door, the three men trapped inside had suffocated from the toxic fumes and died.

America's space program was halted for one and a half years, while improvements were made to the *Apollo* capsules. The next manned Apollo flight was launched on October 11, 1968—with a redesigned capsule that allowed emergency access.

• A TRAGIC LANDING •

The first person killed during an actual spaceflight was Russian cosmonaut Vladimir M. Komarov, commander of the *Soyuz 1* capsule. After successfully completing seventeen Earth orbits, Komarov's single-occupant capsule began its descent sequence. After passing through the atmosphere, the capsule released a parachute to slow its speed. At 23,000 feet, however, the parachute became entangled and collapsed. *Soyuz 1* hit the ground at 200 miles per hour and exploded in flames. Komarov died instantly.

THE SOVIET UNION'S *SOYUZ* CAPSULE ▲

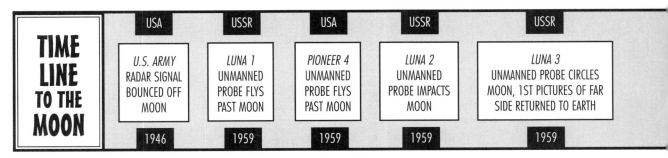

TIME LINE TO THE MOON	USA	USSR	USA	USSR	USSR
	U.S. ARMY RADAR SIGNAL BOUNCED OFF MOON	LUNA 1 UNMANNED PROBE FLYS PAST MOON	PIONEER 4 UNMANNED PROBE FLYS PAST MOON	LUNA 2 UNMANNED PROBE IMPACTS MOON	LUNA 3 UNMANNED PROBE CIRCLES MOON, 1ST PICTURES OF FAR SIDE RETURNED TO EARTH
	1946	1959	1959	1959	1959

• DEATH IN SPACE •

The only astronauts to die in space to date were the three cosmonauts aboard the *Soyuz 11* space capsule. On June 6, 1971, after a successful launch and docking with the *Salyut 1* space station, the trio completed a twenty-four-day orbital mission. While returning to Earth, however, a valve ruptured aboard their spacecraft, releasing all its oxygen into space.

The capsule sped through Earth's atmosphere and landed on target, but technicians opened the door to find that the three comrades had suffocated in the vacuum of space.

To avoid repeating the tragedy, future *Soyuz* capsules were modified to seat two cosmonauts instead of three, allowing enough room for them to wear pressurized space suits during lift-off and reentry. If *Soyuz 11*'s passengers had been wearing such space suits, they might have survived the rapid depressurization of their cabin.

• A NEAR DISASTER •

After the successful *Apollo 11* and *12* Moon landings, many Americans were no longer impressed by space travel, having forgotten how dangerous space can be. They were jolted back to reality on April 13, 1970, when the *Apollo 13* capsule exploded en route to the Moon.

More than halfway to their destination, the *Apollo 13* crew were performing routine tasks. One astro-

AN OXYGEN TANK EXPLOSION CRIPPLED THE *APOLLO 13* CAPSULE ▲

naut activated a switch that stirred the oxygen stored in tanks attached to the spacecraft. No one realized that the tanks' wiring had been damaged weeks before lift-off, and the stirring procedure created a spark that set the flammable oxygen on fire.

USA	USA	USA	USA	USA	USA
RANGER 3 UNMANNED PROBE IMPACTS MOON	*RANGER 4* UNMANNED PROBE IMPACTS FAR SIDE OF THE MOON	*RANGER 5* UNMANNED PROBE SENDS SEISMIC DATA FROM MOON	*RANGER 6* UNMANNED PROBE SENDS TV PICTURES OF MOON TO EARTH	*RANGER 7* UNMANNED PROBE SENDS 1ST CLOSE-UP PHOTOS	*RANGER 9* UNMANNED PROBE IMPACTS MOON ON TARGET
1962	1962	1962	1964	1964	1965

In an instant, most of the spaceship's electrical and operating systems were destroyed. What was worse, the astronauts looked out the capsule window to see their precious oxygen supply escaping into space. There was no longer any hope of landing on the Moon; the *Apollo 13* astronauts would be lucky just to get back home alive.

With their space capsule destroyed, the astronauts moved into the only other compartment capable of supporting life: the lunar lander module. Unfortunately, the module was designed to support two men instead of three, so no one was certain whether there would be enough water, air, and electricity for the crew to survive the journey home.

APOLLO 13 ASTRONAUTS HAISE, LOVELL, AND SWIGERT AFTER THEIR ORDEAL IN SPACE ▲

With ground controllers radioing commands to the astronauts, they lowered the temperature of the cabin to just above freezing, in order to conserve power. Each man was rationed just 6 ounces of water each day. And the *Apollo* capsule continued on to the Moon, using the satellite's gravitational field to fling itself earthward.

The capsule survived reentry by the narrowest of margins. But space scientists were quick to call the mission a success, because the accident in space had taught them much about dealing with unexpected disasters so many miles from Earth. To learn more about the *Apollo 13* mission, visit: http://nssdc.gsfc.nasa.gov/planetary/lunar/ap13acc.html

USSR	USSR	USA	USA	USSR	USSR
LUNA 9 UNMANNED PROBE MAKES 1ST SOFT LANDING ON MOON	*LUNA 10* UNMANNED PROBE MAKES 1ST LUNAR ORBIT	*SURVEYOR 1* UNMANNED PROBE SOFT-LANDS ON MOON, TESTS SOIL	*LUNAR ORBITER* UNMANNED PROBE PHOTOGRAPHS LANDING SITES FROM LUNAR ORBIT	*LUNA 11* UNMANNED PROBE ORBITS MOON	*LUNA 12* UNMANNED PROBE ORBITS MOON
1966	1966	1966	1966	1966	1966

• THE CHALLENGER DISASTER •

January 28, 1986, was to be the beginning of a new era in spaceflight. Aboard the Space Shuttle *Challenger* was a new kind of astronaut: a schoolteacher from New Hampshire named Christa McAuliffe.

McAuliffe had been selected from 11,000 applicants as part of a "Schoolteachers in

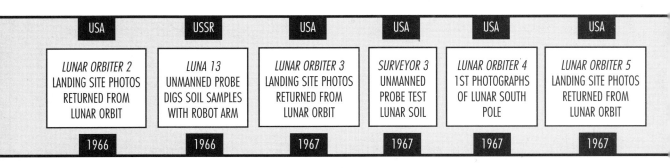

USA	USSR	USA	USA	USA	USA
LUNAR ORBITER 2 LANDING SITE PHOTOS RETURNED FROM LUNAR ORBIT	*LUNA 13* UNMANNED PROBE DIGS SOIL SAMPLES WITH ROBOT ARM	*LUNAR ORBITER 3* LANDING SITE PHOTOS RETURNED FROM LUNAR ORBIT	*SURVEYOR 3* UNMANNED PROBE TEST LUNAR SOIL	*LUNAR ORBITER 4* 1ST PHOTOGRAPHS OF LUNAR SOUTH POLE	*LUNAR ORBITER 5* LANDING SITE PHOTOS RETURNED FROM LUNAR ORBIT
1966	1966	1967	1967	1967	1967

Space" program. Although she had had no flight experience before becoming an astronaut, she'd won the opportunity to broadcast live school lessons from space to classrooms across America.

Unfortunately, the cold January weather at the launch site had frozen an important part of the shuttle's solid rocket boosters: a rubber O-ring connected to the main fuel tank. The rubber seal shrank after freezing, creating a gap that allowed burning fuel to escape as the shuttle roared skyward. Seventy-three seconds after lift-off, *Challenger* exploded in a ball of flame, killing all seven astronauts on board.

The entire shuttle fleet was grounded for two years eight months while technicians examined the cause of the crash. Remaining shuttles were improved to make a repeat of the accident unlikely. And a new shuttle, *Endeavour*, was built to replace *Challenger*.

Naming a new shuttle. Soon after the *Challenger* disaster, NASA began construction on a new shuttle to replace the destroyed orbiter. It was decided that the replacement, like the other shuttles in the fleet, should be named after a famous historical exploring ship.

To honor the teacher who was to bring space science to classrooms around the country, Congress directed NASA to let America's schoolchildren choose a name for the new shuttle. A nationwide contest was held, divided into two categories: K–6th and 7–12th grades. Each of over 6,000 participating classrooms submitted names, along with research projects showing why their choice was significant.

SCHOOLTEACHERS IN SPACE

After the *Challenger* disaster, NASA halted its "Schoolteachers in Space" program, declaring the risks of space travel too great for everyday citizens. Now, twelve years later, NASA is preparing to fly teachers into space once again. Barbara Morgan, an elementary schoolteacher from McCall, Idaho, has been selected to enter the astronaut program. After she completes a year of training in 1999, Morgan will be assigned a future shuttle mission. Aboard the shuttle, Morgan will fulfill Christa McAuliffe's dream: broadcasting lessons from space to classrooms across America.

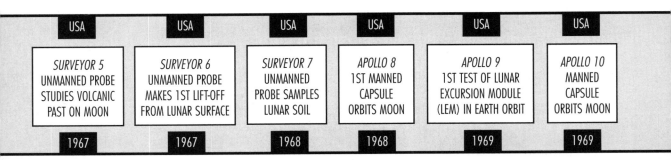

USA	USA	USA	USA	USA	USA
SURVEYOR 5 UNMANNED PROBE STUDIES VOLCANIC PAST ON MOON	*SURVEYOR 6* UNMANNED PROBE MAKES 1ST LIFT-OFF FROM LUNAR SURFACE	*SURVEYOR 7* UNMANNED PROBE SAMPLES LUNAR SOIL	*APOLLO 8* 1ST MANNED CAPSULE ORBITS MOON	*APOLLO 9* 1ST TEST OF LUNAR EXCURSION MODULE (LEM) IN EARTH ORBIT	*APOLLO 10* MANNED CAPSULE ORBITS MOON
1967	1967	1968	1968	1969	1969

The winning name, *Endeavour*, was also the most popular choice. *Endeavour* was the name of the ship used by the British explorer Captain James Cook to explore the South Pacific between 1768 and 1772, eventually sailing around the entire globe. Other popular names included *Resolution* (another of Cook's ships), *Victoria* (the first ship to sail around the world), *Adventure, Meteor, Pathfinder, Phoenix*, and *Victory*.

• A SPACE WALK TO DANGER •

For every mission success or disaster, there have been plenty of close calls in space. On July 17, 1990, nearing the end of a successful space walk, cosmonauts Antoly Solovov and Alexander N. Balandin discovered that their return hatchway wouldn't seal properly—preventing access to the *Mir* space station's interior. After six hours in space, neither man had much oxygen left in his spacesuit. With no other options, they hooked their life support systems to an emergency oxygen tank outside the station and carefully crawled to another entryway. This time, the airlock's outer hatch sealed properly, allowing the men to reenter the station in the nick of time.

• THE ASTRONAUTS' MEMORIAL •

NASA has erected a monument to all of America's lost astronauts at Kennedy Space Center in Florida. The monument, called the Space Mirror, is a 42-by-50-foot wall of black granite with the astronauts' names carved into its surface. The 37-ton slab sits on a turntable and rotates with the Sun, whose light shines through each astronaut's name. At night or on cloudy days, each name is lit up with spotlights.

Many deceased astronauts and cosmonauts have been given a far more permanent memorial: Craters on the Moon have been named after them. The International Astronomical Union has also named seven asteroids after the deceased *Challenger* astronauts: Francis R. "Dick" Scobee, Michael J. Smith, Judith A. Resnik, Ellison S. Onizuka, Ronald E. McNair, Gregory B. Jarvis, and Sharon Christa McAuliffe. For more information on the Space Mirror Memorial, visit: http://www.amfcse.org/content/thespace.htm

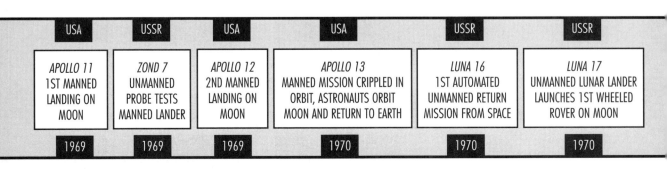

USA	USSR	USA	USA	USSR	USSR
APOLLO 11 1ST MANNED LANDING ON MOON	*ZOND 7* UNMANNED PROBE TESTS MANNED LANDER	*APOLLO 12* 2ND MANNED LANDING ON MOON	*APOLLO 13* MANNED MISSION CRIPPLED IN ORBIT, ASTRONAUTS ORBIT MOON AND RETURN TO EARTH	*LUNA 16* 1ST AUTOMATED UNMANNED RETURN MISSION FROM SPACE	*LUNA 17* UNMANNED LUNAR LANDER LAUNCHES 1ST WHEELED ROVER ON MOON
1969	1969	1969	1970	1970	1970

Unmanned Space Probes

How does NASA decide which missions need astronauts and which should use unmanned probes? At this point, the agency uses robotic craft on long-term or dangerous missions, and astronauts on near-Earth missions that benefit from on-the-spot decision making. In the future, however, as computers grow more sophisticated, intelligent probes may explore space without the need for human assistance at all.

• BACK TO THE MOON AT LAST •

NASA launched nine Moon missions during the Apollo program (1968–72), but since then NASA has focused on sending unmanned spacecraft to the remainder of the solar system, leaving more than 75 percent of the Moon unexplored. On January 25, 1994, that focus changed: NASA launched *Clementine* and returned to the Moon at last.

Clementine was the first in a series of missions planned for Earth's nearest neighbor. Designed to map the lunar surface (and near-Earth asteroid 1620 Geographos), the space probe achieved lunar orbit a month after launch and began returning images to Earth. Two months later, however, *Clementine* malfunctioned, firing a thruster until it used up all its fuel and spun out of control. The spaceship failed to complete its planned mission. For more information on *Clementine*, visit:
http://nssdc.gsfc.nasa.gov/planetary/lunar/clementine1.html

USA	USA	USSR	USA	USA	USSR
APOLLO 14 3RD MANNED LANDING ON MOON	*APOLLO 15* 4TH MANNED LANDING ON MOON	*LUNA 20* UNMANNED LANDER RETURNS MOONROCKS TO USSR	*APOLLO 16* 5TH MANNED LANDING ON MOON	*APOLLO 17* 6TH MANNED LANDING ON MOON	*LUNA 21* UNMANNED LUNAR ROVER LANDS ON MOON
1971	1971	1971	1972	1972	1973

• PROSPECTING FOR WATER •

For more than a century, science fiction writers have fantasized about building a manned lunar colony. After all, the Moon is only 239,000 miles away—close compared to the vast reaches of space. What's more, the Moon's low gravity should make colony construction fairly easy. Not only could large objects be moved with ease, but large quantities of raw materials could be mined directly from the lunar soil. The only element missing is water—a resource too important and expensive to transport from Earth.

When *Clementine* began its mapping of the lunar surface, early data indicated the possible presence of large amounts of ice at the Moon's poles—enough ice, perhaps, to supply lunar astronauts with a billion tons of water. Unfortunately, the *Clementine* mission failed before the discovery could be confirmed. Now, at last, a new probe is returning to the Moon, and this time its mission is to prospect for water.

On January 5, 1998, NASA launched the *Lunar Prospector.* Flying sixty-three miles above the lunar surface, the unmanned probe will map terrain and search for ice for an entire year. Water-detection sensors aboard the craft are sensitive enough to scan the different energies of individual neutrons and uncover even microscopic amounts of frozen ice buried several feet under the lunar soil.

Thus far, preliminary data have confirmed that water ice exists at the Moon's north and south poles. It is hoped that *Lunar Prospector* will help pave the way for future manned missions. If enough Moon ice is discovered, *Prospector* may help pinpoint the best spot to build a lunar space colony. For more information on the *Lunar Prospector* mission, visit:
http://lunar.arc.nasa.gov

For more information on the possibility of lunar ice, visit:
http://nssdc.gsfc.nasa.gov/planetary/ice/ice_moon.html

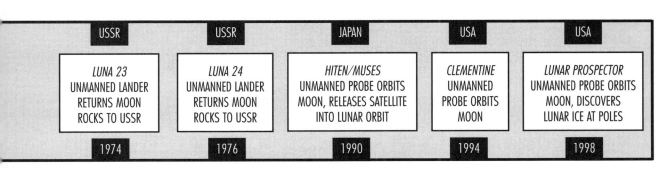

USSR	USSR	JAPAN	USA	USA
LUNA 23 UNMANNED LANDER RETURNS MOON ROCKS TO USSR	LUNA 24 UNMANNED LANDER RETURNS MOON ROCKS TO USSR	HITEN/MUSES UNMANNED PROBE ORBITS MOON, RELEASES SATELLITE INTO LUNAR ORBIT	CLEMENTINE UNMANNED PROBE ORBITS MOON	LUNAR PROSPECTOR UNMANNED PROBE ORBITS MOON, DISCOVERS LUNAR ICE AT POLES
1974	1976	1990	1994	1998

• A RETURN TO THE RED PLANET •

When *Pathfinder* landed on Mars during the summer of 1997, it did more than signal NASA's first return to the Red Planet in more than twenty years. *Pathfinder* was the first big test of NASA's new mandate to design "cheaper, better, and faster" space missions than ever before. In 1975, when two *Viking* spacecraft touched down on Mars, their descent through the atmosphere was slowed by large retro-rockets. *Pathfinder* (built at a fraction of the cost of the *Viking* landers) couldn't afford to carry much weight or fuel, so engineers used Martian gravity itself to "aerobrake" the probe, reducing its speed from 17,000 to 840 miles per hour.

MARS PATHFINDER BOUNCES TO A SAFE LANDING ▲

At that speed, *Pathfinder* could safely release a parachute to slow its descent further. One second before impact (about 100 feet above the ground), three tiny nozzles fired, bringing the probe to a momentary standstill. From that point, *Pathfinder* dropped to the planet surface and bounced fifteen times before coming to a stop. In the past, even a single bounce might have destroyed a mission, but *Pathfinder*'s lander was encased in protective air bags and was able to survive the impact safely. For more information on the *Mars Pathfinder* mission, visit: http://mars.jpl.nasa.gov/default.html

• AN EXPLORER NAMED *SOJOURNER* •

After *Pathfinder* bounced to a bumpy landing on the Martian surface, its air bags deflated and unfolded like flower petals, revealing a small, six-wheeled vehicle called *Sojourner*. The 1-foot-tall, 2-foot-long robot explorer eased its way down a ramp and began to roam the Martian surface, taking pictures of rocks and terrain and analyzing the red Martian soil's chemistry.

In the past, American astronauts had driven a Lunar Rover on the Moon, and the *Viking* landers had scraped the Martian soil, all searching for signs of microscopic life. But *Sojourner* accomplished something new: It was the first vehicle able to explore the surface of another world on its own.

Even though the remote explorer was controlled by radio commands from mission scientists at the Jet Propulsion Laboratory in California, it takes eleven minutes for a single command— traveling at the speed of light— to reach Mars from Earth, and eleven more minutes before a return message can let controllers know whether the original message was received. During those twenty-two-minute gaps, *Sojourner* used a sophisticated system of computer electronics, guidance lasers, gyroscopic stabilizers, and other gadgets designed to give the craft an intelligence of

SOJOURNER BEGINS TO EXPLORE THE MARTIAN SURFACE ▲

its own. During its three-month mission, *Sojourner* and *Pathfinder* transmitted 2.6 billion bits of information to Earth, including more than 16,500 pictures of the Martian terrain.

After the mission was over, NASA renamed the *Pathfinder* lander the Carl Sagan Memorial Station, in honor of the astronomer who played a leading role in sending probes to explore our solar system.

• A SURVEY MISSION TO MARS •

When *Viking 1* and *2* landed on Mars in 1976, their mission was limited to searching for signs of microscopic life forms. Now NASA has sent another probe to the Red Planet (one of several separate Martian missions planned) with a much larger task: to map the entire planet surface, track climate and weather, and search for places to land future missions.

The probe, called *Mars Global Surveyor*, was launched in 1996 and began its two-year orbit of Mars in September 1997. Within the first few days of the mission, *Surveyor* began to transmit pictures of the planet surface with fifty times greater detail than images captured by *Viking*. Astronomers learned that Mars has a magnetic field, which shields the planet from many of the harmful particles that stream from space. This finding has led to speculation that billions of years ago, Mars may have been a lot like Earth, with flowing water and active volcanoes. Astronomers are searching for clues to why Mars appears lifeless today, while Earth is alive with plants and creatures. For more information on *Mars Global Surveyor*, visit: http://mars.jpl.nasa.gov/mgs

• JAPAN'S *PLANET-B* PROBE •

On July 4, 1998, the first anniversary of the American *Pathfinder* mission to Mars, another probe was launched to explore the Red Planet—but not by the United States. Japan's Institute of Space and Astronautical Sciences (ISAS) rocketed its first interplanetary probe into space on a mission to measure Mars's magnetic field and solar wind and to use sound waves to search for water trapped in ice beneath the planet's surface. The Japanese call their probe *Planet-B*, and it was launched aboard a rocket named Nozomi ("hope").

Japan is only the third country (in addition to the United States and Russia) to have launched an interplanetary mission. *Planet-B*, however, carries experiments from many different countries on board, including the United States, Canada, Sweden, and Germany.

• THE GALILEO MISSION •

Few of NASA's space missions have had as many unexpected setbacks or breakthrough discoveries as the *Galileo* probe to Jupiter. The craft completed its primary mission in December 1997, sending 1,800 photos of the Jovian system back to Earth. The *Galileo* mission's milestones include:

1982. *Galileo* is scheduled to be launched on a straight path to Jupiter, but the *Challenger* shuttle disaster forces mission planners to delay the launch.

October 1989. *Galileo* is released from the shuttle *Atlantis*'s cargo bay. The delay has forced engineers to send the spacecraft on a journey through the inner solar system, using the gravity of nearby planets to hurl the probe on a trajectory to Jupiter. In all, *Galileo* will have to travel two and a half billion miles to reach a planet only one-half billion miles away.

February 1990. *Galileo* swings by Venus, using the planet's gravity to slingshot back toward Earth.

December 1990. *Galileo* orbits Earth, using our planet's gravity to make another loop through the inner solar system. Astronomers capture the first images of our home world as viewed by an approaching spacecraft. They also test whether *Galileo*'s instruments can detect biological life from space (they can), since we already know that Earth is covered with living plants and creatures.

1991. Astronomers discover that the many years *Galileo* was delayed before launch caused damage to its high-gain antenna (used to send recorded data back to Earth). Mission engineers are forced to use the low-gain antenna, which can send back only a fraction of the information collected by the spacecraft.

October 1991. *Galileo* becomes the first spacecraft to encounter an asteroid, flying by Gaspra. Astronomers develop new methods of data compression to collect information from the low-gain antenna.

GALILEO IS RELEASED FROM SHUTTLE *ATLANTIS'S* CARGO BAY ▲

SPACE PIONEERS

Galileo Galilei (1564–1642) lived in an age when everyday people held many false beliefs about the universe—that the Sun revolves around the Earth, for example. In 1608, however, a Dutch man named Hans Lippershey invented the telescope, and Galileo began to study the stars and planets. He discovered many new stars and proved that the solar system was not made of perfect globes (as was believed) but was filled with worlds of craters, mountains, and valleys. Most important, Galileo discovered four moons orbiting Jupiter. If moons could orbit Jupiter instead of the Earth, then the Earth need not be the center of the universe. Galileo spent many years fighting for this new view of the universe. As he grew older, however, he went blind by studying the Sun and ended his days in darkness.

GALILEO GALILEI

August 1993. *Galileo* passes another asteroid, Ida, and discovers that asteroids can have miniature moons of their own. Ida's small companion is given the name Dactyl.

July 1994. Astronomers Eugene Shoemaker and David Levy discover a comet about to strike Jupiter's surface. *Galileo* gives Earth a close-up look at the impact of comet Shoemaker-Levy 9.

ASTEROID IDA ▲

December 1995. *Galileo* arrives at Jupiter and releases a probe into the turbulent atmosphere. The probe deploys a parachute and floats downward, buffeted about by Jupiter's intense wind currents. Astronomers detect lightning in Jupiter's atmosphere. Nearly an hour after transmitting detailed data about the interior of the atmosphere, the probe is destroyed by 3,400°F heat near the planet's surface.

1996. Astronomers compare new images of Io's surface with those captured by *Voyager* and discover that the moon's surface is constantly remade by volcanic eruptions.

1997. *Galileo* images a complex network of fractured ice on Europa's surface, suggesting the presence of a deep global ocean on this moon of Jupiter. Complex organic molecules may be present in waters washing through the fractured ice.

April 1998. *Galileo* discovers a new ring rotating in a "backward" orbit, opposite the direction in which Jupiter and its moons spin. This may be the only ring of its kind in the solar system.

You can follow *Galileo*'s daily progress and view images sent back to Earth on the mission's Web site: http://www.jpl.nasa.gov/galileo

• EUROPA AND THE SEARCH FOR LIFE •

Because life on Earth first evolved in the ocean, scientists believe that planets with water offer the best chance to discover extraterrestrial life. Although no other planets have been found with oceans like our own, one nearby satellite is surprisingly similar to Earth: Jupiter's moon Europa. Astronomers believe that Europa is a watery world covered by an icy layer, very similar to the Antarctic region at the Earth's South Pole.

Billions of years ago, Jupiter may have been hot enough to heat Europa's oceans, creating a world not too different from our own. As the planet cooled and Europa became encased in ice, any life that formed may have continued to survive. Even today, Jupiter's strong gravity pulls and tugs at Europa's orbit, creating undersea volcanoes that may heat the water beneath the icy surface.

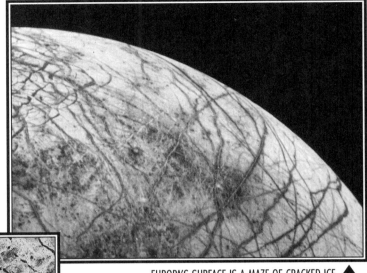

EUROPA'S SURFACE IS A MAZE OF CRACKED ICE ▲

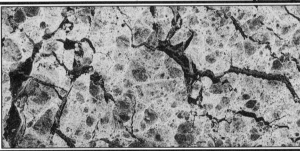

ANTARCTIC ICE MAY PROVIDE CLUES TO LIFE ON EUROPA ▲

NASA is planning a series of space probes to explore these extraterrestrial riddles. The *Ice Clipper* mission will drop a heavy weight onto Europa's surface, then dip down close enough to capture pieces of ice thrown into the atmosphere by the impact. By studying the ice up close, scientists hope to answer the question whether life exists beneath the frozen surface. If organic molecules are detected, NASA may send a probe that lands on Europa's surface, drills through the ice, and explores the undersea regions directly.

In the years before these probes are launched, NASA may test their plans by drilling through Antarctica itself. Algae and other microbes have already been discovered beneath the Antarctic ice, surviving in harsh conditions that may be similar to those found on Mars and Europa. For more information on the *Galileo* Europa mission, visit: http://www.jpl.nasa.gov/galileo/gem/gem1.html

• THE LAST OF THE GIANT SPACESHIPS •

On October 22, 1997, an international team of excited space scientists watched as the last of the "giant spaceships" blasted off from Cape Canaveral. They were watching *Cassini*,

SPACE PIONEERS

Giovanni Domenico Cassini (1625–1712), a brilliant observational astronomer, discovered four of Saturn's moons, as well as the gap in Saturn's rings that today bears his name (the Cassini division). Cassini was the first of four generations of Cassinis who supervised the Paris Observatory over a combined total of 120 years.

GIOVANNI CASSINI

a deep-space probe beginning a seven-year, 2.2-billion-mile voyage to Saturn.

Cassini is considered the last of the "old-style" spaceships because it is large (weighing more than six tons) and contains a dozen different sensors and experiments. It is an entire mission in a single craft. Instead of using one large probe, "new-style" space missions will use several small probes, each launched separately and with a special purpose. This is considered a safer approach, because if something goes wrong with any of the spacecraft, the entire mission will not be jeopardized.

Although it may be the last of its kind, *Cassini* will be the first spacecraft ever launched into Saturn's orbit. It will also be the first space mission to send a probe to the surface of another planet's moon: In November 2004, the *Huygens* probe will detach from *Cassini* and plummet toward Saturn's largest moon, Titan. The *Huygens* probe will take 500 pictures on

CASSINI WILL BE THE FIRST SPACECRAFT TO ORBIT SATURN ▲

the way down, but no one is certain what it will find on the moon's surface. Titan is one of the only bodies in the solar system with its own atmosphere, and its surface may contain oceans of liquid methane or a mantle of methane ice. It is a world that offers much to discover and explore. For more information on the *Cassini* mission, visit:
http://www.jpl.nasa.gov/cassini

SPACE PIONEERS

Christiaan Huygens (1629–95) was a physicist who invented tools to improve the science of astronomy. He developed a method for polishing glass that made telescopes see farther than ever before. He also invented the clock pendulum, which improved the accuracy of timepieces and aided in the computation of celestial orbits. Using these new tools, Huygens discovered the rings of Saturn and its largest moon, Titan.

CHRISTIAAN HUYGENS

• PAW PRINTS ON SATURN •

As *Cassini* streaks on its seven-year voyage to Saturn, it brings with it some unusual Earthly cargo: a computer disk containing hundreds of thousands of signatures, the paw prints of dogs and cats, and the footprints of babies.

The digitized material was collected by the Planetary Society in order to give everyday people a way to journey into space. Also on board are signed letters from the two astronomers for whom the mission is named: A 1690 letter from Giovanni Domenico Cassini and a 1684 letter from Christiaan Huygens.

Once *Cassini* has reached Saturn and completed its four-year mission, scientists expect the craft to orbit the planet for centuries. Even though the computer disk was not sent as a message to aliens, if E.T. should ever intercept the probe, he will have a record of the Earth creatures who helped send *Cassini* on its way!

• EXPLORING SPACE IN A BALLOON •

There's more to planetary exploration than orbiting a robotic probe around a distant world. Whenever possible, space scientists try to land on a planet's surface and explore the surrounding terrain. Landers, rovers, and surface probes have already been sent to the

Moon, Mars, Venus, and Jupiter. A surface probe will land on Saturn's moon Titan in the first years of the twenty-first century. And, in the future, NASA may deploy a new kind of planetary explorer: hot air balloons.

Hot air balloons offer a distinct advantage over stationary landers or rovers: They can literally fly around the world, enabling astronomers to track weather patterns, atmosphere, and surface conditions to search for the best locations for landing future missions. In addition, hot air balloons may be the only way to explore gas giants such as Jupiter and Saturn, whose strong gravity would destroy any probe that attempted to land on the surface. For more information about JPL's *aerobot* program, visit: http://telerobotics.jpl.nasa.gov/aerobot

• *PIONEER 10* SAYS GOOD-BYE •

The *Pioneer 10* probe was launched in 1972 on a twenty-one-month mission to Jupiter. Along the way to the giant gas, *Pioneer 10* recorded many firsts, including the first close-up pictures of the asteroid belt and the first detailed pictures of Jupiter itself. *Pioneer 10* was also the first spacecraft to use another planet's gravity to boost its speed.

Now, twenty-five years later, *Pioneer 10* is poised to become the first spacecraft to leave the solar system. Already 6.2 billion miles from Earth, the probe has not yet crossed the heliopause but is speeding toward Aldebaran, a star sixty-eight light-years away. Getting to Aldebaran will probably take another two million years, but scientists expect *Pioneer 10* to arrive at its destination safely.

A special gold-plated plaque attached to the spaceship shows what humans looks like, *Pioneer 10*'s point of origin (Earth), the probe's flight trajectory, and the Sun's position in the Milky Way. If *Pioneer 10* is ever intercepted by extraterrestrial creatures, they should know something about how far the little craft has flown and the beings who launched it upon its journey. For more information on the *Pioneer 10* mission, visit: http://www.lerc.nasa.gov/WWW/PAO/html/pioneer.htm

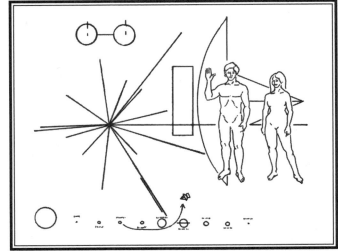

THE *PIONEER 10* PLAQUE IS A GREETING FROM EARTH ▲

HOW WOULD YOU SAY HELLO TO AN EXTRATERRESTRIAL?

It has often been said that "music is the universal language," but how would you say hello to an extraterrestrial? Since no life has ever been discovered beyond the Earth, it's difficult to imagine what communication with an alien race might be like. But astronomers realize that, no matter where they may live in the universe, all creatures share the same physical laws. The formulas that describe elementary particles and the geometry of space must be familiar to all intelligent beings. If there is one "universal" language, it is probably based upon mathematics.

• *VOYAGER* SAYS HELLO •

Two other spacecraft besides *Pioneer 10* are speeding their way out of the solar system: *Voyager 1* and *Voyager 2*, launched in 1977 to explore Jupiter and Saturn. Like *Galileo*, the *Voyager* probes were so successful that their mission was extended (in this case, to include a flyby of Uranus and Neptune).

On November 12, 1980, *Voyager 1* flew by Saturn, using the planet's gravity to swing out of the ecliptic plane. Today, the small spaceship is many billions of miles above the solar system. After completing its tour of the outer planets, *Voyager 2* also left the solar system. Both *Voyager* spacecraft will continue to send signals to Earth for another twenty-five years. Even after they have fallen silent, however, *Voyager 1* and *2* will have one more message to deliver: a two-hour recording of sounds and pictures from Earth.

Like *Pioneer,* the *Voyager* spacecraft have plaques attached showing where they have come from and how to play the messages inside. Contained on *Voyager's* disk are 118 photographs; 90 minutes of music; human greetings in nearly 60 languages; the sound of rainfall, oceans, whales, and animals; and a sampling of other sounds from the evolutionary history of our planet.

There is also a message from Jimmy Carter, U.S. president when the crafts were launched: "This is a present from a small distant world, a token of our sounds, our science, our images, our music and our feelings . . . this record represents our hope and our determination, and our good will in a vast and awesome universe." For more information on the *Voyager* missions, visit: http://vraptor.jpl.nasa.gov/voyager/voyager.html

ULYSSES IS THE FIRST SPACECRAFT TO ORBIT OUTSIDE THE ECLIPTIC PLANE OF THE PLANETS ▲

• A PROBE TO THE SUN •

One of the most unusual of all space probes is *Ulysses*, launched from the Space Shuttle's cargo bay in 1990 on a five-year mission to study the Sun.

Ulysses actually began its journey heading away from the Sun, toward Jupiter. When it reached the giant planet, the solar probe looped around and changed direction, using Jupiter's strong gravitational field to fling itself out of the ecliptic plane.

In 1994, *Ulysses* passed underneath the Sun's southern pole, using the Sun's gravity to swing northward. By 1995, the probe had passed over the Sun's northern pole, and looped back toward Jupiter. *Ulysses* will complete its next orbit and return to the Sun in the year 2000.

It is the only spacecraft that has ever orbited outside the ecliptic plane of the planets. For more information on the *Ulysses* mission, visit: http://ulysses.jpl.nasa.gov

• FLYING INTO THE FUTURE •

In the winter of 1998, NASA will launch the first of a new generation of spaceships, *Deep Space 1 (DS1)*. *DS1* is designed to test twelve new technologies, sending spacecraft farther and faster into space than ever before.

Chief among these new technologies is a new kind of propulsion system called an "ion drive." The ion drive uses xenon gas to generate electronically charged particles in a magnetic field around the spacecraft. If all goes as planned, ion drives will propel *DS1* ten times faster than conventional rocket engines.

For decades, the concept of ion propulsion existed only in science fiction. *DS1* will be a sci-fi spaceship in another way: It will have artificial intelligence (AI) on board. Using a powerful on-board computer, the ship will be able to navigate to distant asteroids and planets without any assistance from engineers on Earth. The day may arrive when space probes launched on deep-space missions radio home only after completing their tasks. To learn more about advanced propulsion systems, visit: http://www.lerc.nasa.gov/WWW/PAO/warp.htm

Exploring Space From Earth

It's not necessary to travel into space to explore the universe. Since ancient times, humans have charted the stars and studied the motion of the heavens from Earth. Today's astronomers are using sophisticated new telescopes to reveal the wonders of space as never before. And we should never forget that pieces of space come "knocking" on Earth's door . . . as meteors that come crashing to the ground.

• SPACE CALENDARS MADE OF STONE •

In ancient times, advanced cultures looked to the stars and created complex astronomical calendars to mark out the year. One of the most impressive and mysterious of these stone calendars is a gigantic monument found in Salisbury Plain, England, called Stonehenge.

Stonehenge, which dates back several thousand years, was probably built by an order of Welsh and British priests called druids. Scientists believe the monument's ring of pillars and high vertical stones marks out the summer solstice, since stars line up at precise intervals visible between pillars at that time of year. Altogether, fifty individual stones line up with the Sun and Moon at various conjunctions throughout the year. To see images of Stonehenge's celestial calendar, visit: http://www.intel.com/cpc/explore/stonehenge

AMERICA'S STONEHENGE

America has constructed its own version of Stonehenge on the University of Missouri campus. To learn more about this project, visit:
http://www.umr.edu/~stonehen

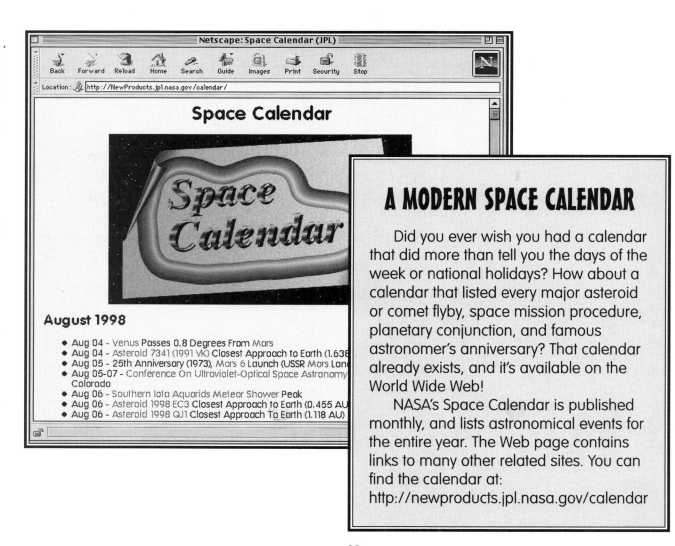

A MODERN SPACE CALENDAR

Did you ever wish you had a calendar that did more than tell you the days of the week or national holidays? How about a calendar that listed every major asteroid or comet flyby, space mission procedure, planetary conjunction, and famous astronomer's anniversary? That calendar already exists, and it's available on the World Wide Web!

NASA's Space Calendar is published monthly, and lists astronomical events for the entire year. The Web page contains links to many other related sites. You can find the calendar at:
http://newproducts.jpl.nasa.gov/calendar

• EYES IN THE SKY •

When we look up into the night sky, we see only a tiny fraction of the universe. Using the naked eye, the farthest visible star is only 2 million light-years away. Since light from a star two million light-years away takes two million years to reach us, looking at the stars is actually looking backward into time. With telescopes, however, we can see objects fifteen million light-years away—all the way to the edge of the universe. We can see all the way back to the beginning of creation.

• AN AGE OF TELESCOPES •

Ever since telescopes were invented (by Dutch scientist Hans Lippershey in 1608), astronomers have worked to improve them. The first telescopes had 4-inch lenses. Modern telescopes are 100 times larger. (The Keck Telescope, the world's largest, is almost 400 inches across.) The larger the telescope, the better its ability to gather light and see distant objects.

Today, giant telescopes are being designed and built all over the world. They have made some amazing discoveries about our universe. These discoveries include:

- A huge black hole lies at the center of our galaxy.
- The Milky Way is attracting and absorbing other galaxies.
- Our galaxy is being drawn toward some mysterious point in the universe, dubbed "the Great Attractor."
- The Great Attractor itself appears to be drawn toward an unknown, even greater gravitational source.
- Evidence of the radiation caused by the Big Bang has been detected.
- Evidence has been found of the mysteriously invisible "dark matter" that may account for 99 percent of the universe.

• EARTH'S SHRINKING TELESCOPES •

Even though today's telescopes are bigger than in the past, they are actually shrinking in their ability to see distant stars. Why? The answer lies in a phenomenon known as "light pollution."

Light pollution is a product of Earth's growing population. As cities expand into previously unpopulated areas, thousands of new lights add brightness to the nighttime sky. Due to this scattered light, telescopes that once peered through pitch-black skies are able to see fewer distant stars than in the past.

• CONNECT-THE-DISHES •

Astronomers have found ways to improve telescopes without building larger dishes or lenses. By combining the data collected from several separate telescopes, they can see the universe as if they were peering through a single telescope hundreds of miles wide!

Astronomers are using this technique to see details of the universe that would have been impossible to photograph just a few years ago. In December 1997, a network of six radio telescopes photographed an exploding black hole in the constellation Aquila. The explosion sent streams of super-hot gas millions of miles out into space at a speed close to the speed of light. To see a collection of Hubble Space Telescope images, visit: http://oposite.stsci.edu/pubinfo/pictures.html

• AN EYE IN ORBIT •

When you look up into the sky, the stars seem to twinkle, an effect caused by the distortion of Earth's atmosphere. People often make wishes on twinkling stars, but if astronomers had a wish it would be to get a clear view of the stars without the distortion and dimming effects of our planet's protective shroud. On April 24, 1990, they finally got their wish when the Hubble Space Telescope (HST) was launched into Earth orbit. The HST isn't Earth's largest telescope, but because it views the heavens from space, it doesn't need to be. Hubble has photographed the clearest pictures of deep space ever taken, peering as far away as the edge of the universe. For more information about the Hubble Space Telescope, visit: http://www.stsci.edu

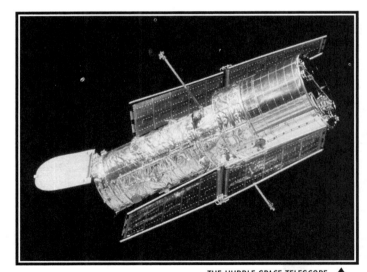

THE HUBBLE SPACE TELESCOPE ▲

The telescope that needed glasses. After the Hubble Space Telescope was launched, its first images were very blurry. Astronomers traced the problem to a flaw in the shape of the telescope's mirror (a problem that should have been discovered and fixed *before* the telescope was launched into space).

To repair Hubble, astronomers needed to give the telescope a special pair of glasses. In 1993, shuttle astronauts performed a series of space walks to add optics that would correct Hubble's blurry vision. Since then, the telescope has revealed our universe as never before. Its many breakthroughs include:

- the discovery of Pluto's moon, Charon
- evidence of black holes at the center of galaxies
- two spiral galaxies crashing into each other
- the birth of stars
- the death of stars (exploding at millions of miles per hour)
- weather tracking on other planets in the solar system
- the edge of the universe itself

ASTRONAUTS REPAIR THE HUBBLE SPACE TELESCOPE IN ORBIT ▲

• A TELESCOPE THAT FLIES THE SKIES •

Another kind of telescope combines the best features of ground-based observatories and the Hubble Space Telescope: the Kuiper Airborne Observatory (KAO).

The KAO is an airplane that has been specially converted into a 6,000-pound infrared telescope with a 36-inch lens. Like Hubble, it can fly above the dimming and distorting effects of Earth's atmosphere, but unlike Hubble it can be easily serviced when it lands on Earth.

The KAO was built in 1974 and makes roughly seventy flights each year, carrying four astronomers and a pilot on board. Among its many achievements, the Kuiper Airborne Observatory has discovered Uranus's rings, Pluto's atmosphere, and water in Jupiter's clouds. To take a virtual tour of the Kuiper Airborne Observatory, visit: http://quest.arc.nasa.gov/lfs/lfs_tour

• HUBBLE'S SEQUEL •

Sometime in the first few years of the twenty-first century, NASA plans to launch Hubble's replacement, the Next Generation Space Telescope (NGST).

The NGST will be assembled in space. Unlike Hubble, it will be placed in an orbit far away from Earth so that even the faint heat generated by our planet doesn't distort its images. It will be much larger than Hubble—so big that the shuttle will have to carry it into orbit in separate pieces.

Astronomers expect the Next Generation Space Telescope to reveal wondrous new details about our universe, sending home pictures of faint, faraway galaxies even as they are born. For more information on the Next Generation Space Telescope, visit: http://ngst.gsfc.nasa.gov

• THE GREAT OBSERVATORIES •

The Hubble Space Telescope is only one of four "great observatories" NASA has scheduled for launch into space. The Compton Gamma Ray Observatory (CGRO) is already in orbit. NASA plans to launch an Advanced X-ray Astrophysics Facility (AXAF) by the end of 1998. A fourth observatory, the Space Infrared Telescope Facility (SIRTF) is currently being designed and is tentatively scheduled for launch in December 2001.

Combined, the four space observatories will be able to return data from most of the electromagnetic spectrum. Hubble is an optical telescope, searching the visible spectrum. CGRO detects gamma rays, a form of high-energy radiation emitted by solar flares, pulsars, quasars, and other deep-space objects. AXAF will search the x-ray spectrum, photographing exploding stars and hot gases at the core of black holes; SIRTF wil observe infrared light, which shows heat (even the heat generated by planets or other objects obscured from sight by dark space matter).

CGRO Web site: http://cossc.gsfc.nasa.gov/cossc/descriptions/cgro.html
SIRTF Web site: http://ssc.ipac.caltech.edu/sirtf
AXAF Web site: http://xrtpub.harvard.edu/pub.html

• THE SEARCH FOR OTHER WORLDS •

One of NASA's newest programs is the Terrestrial Planet Finder (TPF), a search for planets orbiting nearby stars. In the past, detecting planets has been a nearly impossible task, comparable to seeing a speck of dust while staring at a floodlight. The brightness of stars and their distance from Earth make planets invisible to earthbound telescopes. In the past, astronomers have detected extra-solar planets, not by seeing them, but by detecting the gravitational wobbles they produce in stars themselves.

The Terrestrial Planet Finder program hopes to change all that. The TPF is a special type of observatory—an interferometer—made up of several different kinds of telescopes working together to simulate a telescope almost 300 yards wide (nine times larger than Earth's biggest ground-based telescope). To create the sharpest images possible, the TPF will be launched into deep space to orbit the outer part of our solar system, away from the heat and glare of our Sun.

By combining the data collected on different wavelengths outside the visual spectrum, the Terrestrial Planet Finder will screen out any light produced by stars, leaving only the atmospheric heat and gases of orbiting planets. If the TPF succeeds, we earthlings may soon see the first pictures of planets like our own, our closest neighbors in the Milky Way. For more information on the Terrestrial Planet Finder, visit:
http://www.hq.nasa.gov/office/oss/origins/Origins.html

For more on NASA's Exploration of Neighboring Planetary Systems (ExNPS) program, visit:
http://origins.jpl.nasa.gov/missions/terrplfndr.html

• BETTER WAYS TO SEE THE STARS •

The distorting effects of Earth's atmosphere have frustrated stargazers for centuries, but today's astronomers have devised new ways to see the stars more clearly.

By shining two laser beams, one copper-vapor (a green beam) and the other sodium-wavelength (an orange beam), into the Earth's atmosphere, astronomers are able to create points of light that twinkle and shine like stars. Because the light originates from Earth, computers can gauge the amount of distortion caused by the atmosphere and adjust telescopic images to show the stars as if no atmosphere existed at all.

This new science, called "adaptive optics," makes it possible to see things invisible to Earth-based telescopes in the past; for instance, weather patterns on other planets, and the surface features of Saturn's moon Titan (something even the *Voyager* spacecraft couldn't do on their flybys in 1980 and 1981). Even amateur astronomers can now enjoy the added imaging power of adaptive optics: The technology was declassified by the military in 1991, and adaptive optics systems are now available for use with small telescopes.

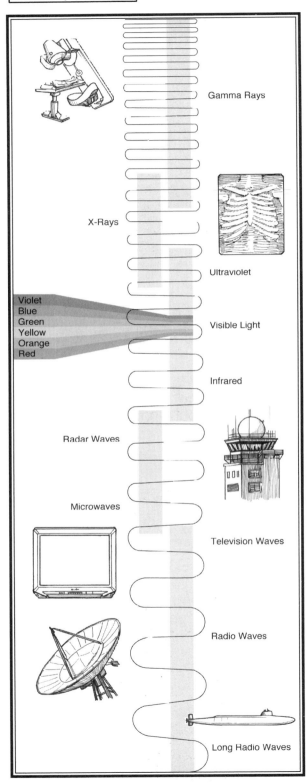

Gamma Rays

X-Rays

Ultraviolet

Violet
Blue
Green
Yellow
Orange
Red

Visible Light

Infrared

Radar Waves

Microwaves

Television Waves

Radio Waves

Long Radio Waves

• THE INVISIBLE SPECTRUM •

Human eyesight is adapted to what is called the "visible spectrum," the portion of the electromagnetic spectrum in which white light is visible. But many other wavelengths of light are invisible to us. Astronomers have developed new telescopes to see across the entire spectrum, revealing the universe in new and exciting ways.

The full spectrum includes:

Gamma rays: Gamma rays can show the heat created by cosmic rays colliding with clouds of gas.

X Rays: X rays, produced by the hot gases surrounding each galaxy, are everywhere throughout the universe.

Ultraviolet light: Ultraviolet light can reveal distant stars hidden behind clouds of inter-stellar gas and other bright stars.

Visible light: Visible light shows us only those stars and gases not obscured by dust or other dark matter.

Infrared light: Infrared light can see through clouds of dust and reveal the very center of our galaxy.

Microwaves: Microwaves measure the tem-perature of the universe, revealing the age of stars and areas of unseen activity.

Radio waves: Radio waves are ideal for long-distance communication, revealing the basic elements (hydrogen, helium, and other gases) that make up the universe.

The future of telescope astronomy promises even more wonders. Scientists hope to one day place a telescope on the far side of the Moon, where it will be shielded from sunlight and from the Earth's reflective glow. Such a telescope might be able to see planets orbiting other stars in detail for the first time.

• THE SOUNDS OF SPACE •

Because sound waves can't travel through the vacuum of space, it is a place of absolute silence. But astronomers plan to listen to the sounds of another world for the first time when *Cassini* reaches Saturn in 2004 and detaches the *Huygens* probe for descent to Titan's surface.

Because Titan is one of the few moons with an atmosphere (it is as large as the planet Mercury), astronomers believe it is possible to hear sounds there. As *Huygens* descends through the clouds, tiny microphones may relay the sounds of lightning and thunder and of the probe's touchdown onto rocks and ice or seas of liquid methane.

Any sounds picked up will be converted into digital information and sent back to Earth through an on-board antenna. If all goes as planned, astronomers will be able to hear the sounds of Titan through an ordinary radio receiver.

• ASTEROID IMPACTS •

Our solar system is filled with hundreds of thousands of asteroids unleashing a constant rain of meteors on all the planets and their moons. Most of these meteors are small enough to disintegrate in the atmosphere, but every so often a large meteorite impacts a planet's surface.

In 1994, astronomers witnessed comet Shoemaker-Levy 9 as it struck the planet Jupiter, sending huge plumes of gas thousands of miles into the atmosphere. Have we had similar impacts here on Earth? The answer is a definite yes. For further information on comet Shoemaker-Levy 9's impact with Jupiter, visit: http://nssdc.gsfc.nasa.gov/planetary/comet.html
For more information on asteroids and comets, visit: http://nssdc.gsfc.nasa.gov/planetary/planets/asteroidpage.html

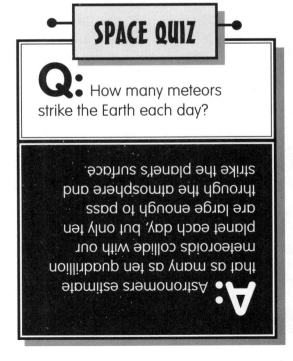

SPACE QUIZ

Q: How many meteors strike the Earth each day?

A: Astronomers estimate that as many as ten quadrillion meteoroids collide with our planet each day, but only ten are large enough to pass through the atmosphere and strike the planet's surface.

• DEATH TO THE DINOSAURS •

Dinosaurs ruled the Earth for 140 million years. Then, almost overnight, they disappeared. What happened? Sixty-five million years ago, a large meteor five to ten miles across slammed into the Earth, creating an impact crater 185 miles wide. The blast was equal to 300 million hydrogen bombs exploding at once (far more than all the nuclear weapons on Earth today)!

The meteor set trees aflame all over the world and threw so much smoke and dust into the atmosphere that the skies grew dark for years. Plants that weren't burned by fire died from lack of sunlight, and soon after so did the plant-eating creatures. This event spelled the end for large meat-eating dinosaurs, who could find nothing left to eat and faded into extinction.

It was at this point that small creatures hiding in the shadows came out into the open. With the death of the dinosaurs, mammals were able to flourish and over millions of years evolved into humans. Our species owes its existence to the destruction caused by a meteor from outer space.

What evidence remains of this terrifying cataclysm? Scientists have found a fine layer of iridium (a mineral rare on Earth but common in meteorites) all over the Earth at the K-T boundary, the layer of rock that marks the point of the dinosaurs' extinction. Using space satellites, astronomers have found the giant meteor's impact crater in what is now the Yucatán peninsula, Mexico. For more information on the Yucatán meteor impact, visit: http://marvel.stsci.edu/exined-html/Impact.html

• AN IMPACT CRATER YOU CAN VISIT •

Twenty-thousand years ago, a 70,000-ton meteor, streaking toward Earth at 45,000 miles per hour, landed near Winslow, Arizona, leaving a mile-wide crater in the dry

desert soil. Upon impact, the 150-foot wide meteor melted sand into glass and killed every living thing for miles around.

Today, the site is called Barringer Meteor Crater and is probably the best example of a meteor impact visible in the world. Every year, thousands of tourists visit the site to witness the awe-some power of an asteroid's impact firsthand! For more information on Barringer Meteor Crater, visit: http://www.hawastsoc.org/solar/cap/earth/meteor.htm

BARRINGER METEOR CRATER, ARIZONA ▲▲

• THE TUNGUSKA FIREBALL •

In 1908, residents of a remote region of the Soviet Union called Tunguska (Siberia) saw a fiery comet streak through the sky. Moments later, the ground shook, knocking people off their feet. The culprit was the Tunguska fireball, a meteor that exploded with the force of a thousand atomic bombs.

Tunguska was such a remote region that scientists didn't visit the impact site for nine-teen years. What they found was one of the worst scenes of destruction ever witnessed: hundreds of square miles of devestation. The entire forest was burned bare and knocked flat to the ground. In 1927, no one was sure what could have caused such destruction.

Today, researchers have found tiny meteorite particles embedded in Tunguska's trees and have calculated that a meteor exploded four miles above the ground, leaving no impact crater. From examining the particles, they know that the meteor came from the far side of our solar system's asteroid belt. For more information on the Tunguska fireball, visit: http://bohp03.bo.infn.it/tunguska96

• WHEN WILL THE NEXT METEOR STRIKE? •

It's only a matter of time before another large meteor strikes the Earth, but when and where will the impact occur? Scientists estimate that there are thousands of meteorites in nearby space that could cause worldwide devastation, but so far only two hundred have been identified and tracked.

In 1996, astronomers spotted an asteroid 1,600 feet wide just four days before it narrowly missed hitting the Earth. If it had struck the planet, the impact would have been equal to all the world's nuclear weapons exploding at once—enough to spell the end of civilization as we know it.

Can anything be done to prevent such a disaster? The answer is yes. Early detection of an asteroid might allow scientists enough time to launch a rocket into space to intercept the meteor and divert it from its collision course. NASA has established a Near-Earth Asteroid Tracking (NEAT) system to identify and catalog comets or asteroids that might pose a danger to Earth (anything larger than a half-mile in diameter). For more information on meteor and comet tracking, visit: http://nssdc.gsfc.nasa.gov/planetary/text/neat_pr.txt

• SEARCH FOR METEORS . . . WITH YOUR RADIO! •

Believe it or not, you can hear passing meteors with nothing more than an FM radio! How? Unlike optical telescopes, radio receivers can detect a wide range of signals, even when it's cloudy or raining outside. With a little practice, you can listen for and track passing meteors—just like a professional astronomer!

To begin, set up an FM receiver outdoors (a car radio will do). If you can position the antenna, try pointing it toward the horizon. Next, tune the dial to any "unoccupied" frequency (a place between radio stations). FM frequencies can be found between 88.1 and 107.9. If you can't find an unoccupied frequency, then choose an FM station whose signal is weakest.

At first, all you will hear is static. But every time a meteor passes, you will hear a little music (or a few words) from another radio station. The radio signals are brief—anywhere from a fraction of a second to several seconds long. If a signal fades in slowly or remains for longer than a few seconds, it's not a meteor.

Meteors don't make sounds by themselves. What you hear is caused by the trail of ionized gas created as a meteor strikes Earth's atmosphere. This gas bounces radio signals—which would normally escape into space—back to Earth.

The best time to listen for meteors is during a meteor shower. (You can check NASA's Space Calendar [see page 82] to find the next expected shower.) At any other time of year, the best time to listen is 6 A.M. If you connect your radio to a tape machine, you don't even have to be there when a meteor passes—just play back the recording to hear the sounds of a universe in motion!

LIFE IN SPACE

Even though humans have flown in space for decades, it remains a dangerous place to live and work. Since astronauts are completely reliant on their space suits, spacecraft, or space stations to survive, safety is still the most essential concern. But years of experience have taught planners a lot about life in orbit, and humankind's continued presence in space is assured.

• WHAT IT TAKES TO BECOME AN ASTRONAUT •

When NASA began its astronaut selection program in 1959, all qualifying candidates were military jet pilots with an extensive knowledge of engineering. Soon after, NASA expanded the range of qualified candidates, accepting applications from civilian pilots with many hours of flying experience. Later, the requirements were changed again to allow nonpilots with academic expertise in biology, medicine, and other sciences into the astronaut program.

Today, the requirements are fairly simple. All Mission Specialist (MS) candidates must be American citizens between 4'10.5" and 6'4" tall. (Pilot candidates must be between 5'4" and 6'4" tall.) Candidates must pass a routine physical test, with blood pressure measuring below 140/90 (in a sitting position). Color vision is required, and eyesight must be correctable to 20/20 (if glasses are required). All candidates must have a bachelor's degree in math, science, or engineering. (In reality, most candidates have advanced college degrees as well.)

Of course, since astronaut requirements have changed in the past, they will probably change again in the future. When traveling into space becomes more commonplace, schoolteachers, artists, writers, and musicians will fly in space, as mission specialists best suited to communicate the joys and wonders of space to nonscientists. For more information on becoming an astronaut, write to:

Astronaut Selection Office
NASA Johnson Space Center
Houston, TX 77058

• IS THERE AN AGE LIMIT FOR ASTRONAUTS? •

Being an astronaut has always been a job for the young. When NASA began its space program, all its astronauts were between twenty-three and forty-one years of age. To this day, no astronaut over the age of sixty-one has flown into space. Yet, if all goes as planned, the future of space travel may be open to senior citizens, too.

Thirty-five years after becoming America's first astronaut to orbit the Earth, John Glenn, at age seventy-seven, has been selected by NASA to fly into space again. Astronaut Glenn will serve as a payload specialist aboard the STS-95 shuttle mission, scheduled for launch October 29, 1998. In orbit, the elderly astronaut will study the effects of weightlessness on bones, muscles, sleep cycles, and aging. Glenn dedicated his mission to senior citizens all over the world.

ASTRONAUT JOHN GLENN FLEW ABOARD THE SHUTTLE AT AGE 77! ▲

• WILL ORDINARY PEOPLE EVER BE ABLE TO FLY IN SPACE? •

For those who spend their lives wishing they could become astronauts, there may be a way to travel into space after all—after death. A private company launching commercial satellites now offers customers a chance to "hitch a ride" into orbit—assuming they're small enough to fit inside a small cylinder a few inches long! Among the famous people whose cremated ashes have already taken the journey into orbit are Gene Roddenberry, the creator of *Star Trek*.

These space pioneers will not orbit the Earth indefinitely, however. Three years after they are launched into orbit, the capsules will fall back into the atmosphere, burning up in a blazing streak across the night sky.

• TRAINING FOR WEIGHTLESSNESS •

An important part of an astronaut's training program is learning how to float in space. Here on Earth, however, there's only one way to simulate weightlessness: flying in an airplane nicknamed the "Vomit Comet." The Vomit Comet is actually an ordinary airplane with all the seats removed. The pilot flies steeply upward, and then changes direction and races toward the ground, making everything—and everybody—inside the plane float in the air for a brief period of time. Before reaching the ground, the pilot changes direction again, racing upward and repeating the maneuver. It's something like a rollercoaster ride in the sky, and many astronauts have found the experience sickening enough for the plane to earn its nickname.

THE ONLY WAY TO EXPERIENCE WEIGHTLESSNESS ON EARTH IS ABOARD THE "VOMIT COMET" ▲

• IS BEING WEIGHTLESS DANGEROUS? •

Living in weightlessness takes some getting used to, but it's not just disorienting to astronauts—it's also dangerous to their health. Why? Humans evolved in Earth's gravity, and living under any other conditions, such as increased gravity or none at all, puts a strain on our bodies. Because the heart doesn't have to work as hard to pump blood in space, it grows weaker. Internal organs like the kidneys or liver can float upward in the body. An astronaut's sense of balance and orientation can fail, making it difficult to know which way is up or down. Bones lose their calcium and break more easily. And muscles shrink in size and weaken, making everyday tasks a tiring experience.

Astronauts must exercise regularly to help their hearts pump harder and their muscles stay strong. Daily diets are adjusted to maintain calcium levels. But even these measures can't counteract the effects of space completely. Astronauts returning to Earth after long periods of weightlessness at first find it difficult to move under Earth's gravity. If people were to live in space for many years, they might never be able to return to the Earth's surface and remain healthy.

• AN INSTANT WAY TO GROW •

One of the more unusual aspects of weightlessness is its effect on an astronaut's height: In space, the spine spreads farther apart, making a person one or two inches taller! The back muscles attached to the spine don't grow any longer, however, so the extra stretching means that most astronauts have a backache during their first few days in orbit. After a while, back muscles stretch enough to make the pain fade away.

The extra height is temporary, however. After the astronauts return to Earth, the effects of gravity collapse the spine again, and all astronauts revert to their normal size.

LIVING IN SPACE CAN MAKE YOU AN INCH OR TWO TALLER!

• LAUNCH PREPARATIONS •

There is a limited period of time—called the "launch window"—during which a spacecraft can be safely launched and successfully complete its mission. Some variables affecting the length of launch windows are weather (extreme cold or cloud cover can delay a launch), the position of orbiting planets or other targets, and solar activity (which might interrupt electronic equipment).

If a space mission is unable to take off during its window, it has a "launch abort." Sometimes an abort will mean flight engineers simply wait for the next available launch window, and other times a spacecraft must be emptied of fuel and prepared for an entirely new mission. If an unmanned spacecraft has already left the ground when a launch abort occurs, it can be destroyed through a special explosive system on board.

WHERE'S THE BEST PLACE TO LAUNCH ON EARTH?

In order for an object to escape Earth orbit, it must travel at least 25,000 miles per hour (7 miles per second). The best way to launch a rocket into space is from Earth's equator, heading east. Why? The Earth spins fastest at the equator, giving rockets an extra push upward and helping them reach their "escape velocity" sooner.

THE ANDROMEDA GALAXY, 2.2 MILLION LIGHT-YEARS AWAY, IS VISIBLE TO THE NAKED EYE. HUBBLE HAS DISCOVERED A DOUBLE NUCLEUS AT ITS CENTER, POSSIBLY THE RESULT OF A SMALLER GALAXY HAVING BEEN ABSORBED BY ANDROMEDA IN THE PAST.

Hubble
Space Telescope

THE HUBBLE SPACE TELESCOPE, ORBITING ABOVE THE EARTH, IS ABLE TO PEER INTO SPACE WITHOUT THE DISTORTION CAUSED BY OUR PLANET'S ATMOSPHERE. HUBBLE HAS TAKEN THE CLEAREST PHOTOGRAPHS OF OUR UNIVERSE EVER SEEN.

THE EAGLE NEBULA: PILLARS OF HYDROGEN AND DUST THAT WILL ONE DAY BECOME STARS. THE TALLEST PILLAR (AT LEFT) IS OVER 3 LIGHT-YEARS HIGH.

SUPERNOVA 1987A RINGS: THE REMAINS OF AN EXPLODED STAR. THE RINGS ARE CAUSED BY EJECTED GAS HEATED BY THE EXPLOSION TO THE POINT OF VISIBILITY

Comets

COMETS ARE LARGE CLUMPS OF ROCK, DUST, AND ICE ORBITING A STAR. IN THIS IMAGE, COMET WEST STREAKS NEAR THE SUN, TRAILING A LONG, GASEOUS TAIL AS HEAT MELTS ITS ICY PARTICLES.

The Sun

OUR SUN IS A FAIRLY ORDINARY YELLOW STAR, BUT THE AWESOME POWER OF ITS NUCLEAR REACTIONS CREATES A STRIKING IMAGE. HUGE STREAMS OF SUPERHEATED GAS CAN LEAP OFF THE SURFACE OF THE SUN HUNDREDS OF THOUSANDS OF MILES INTO SPACE.

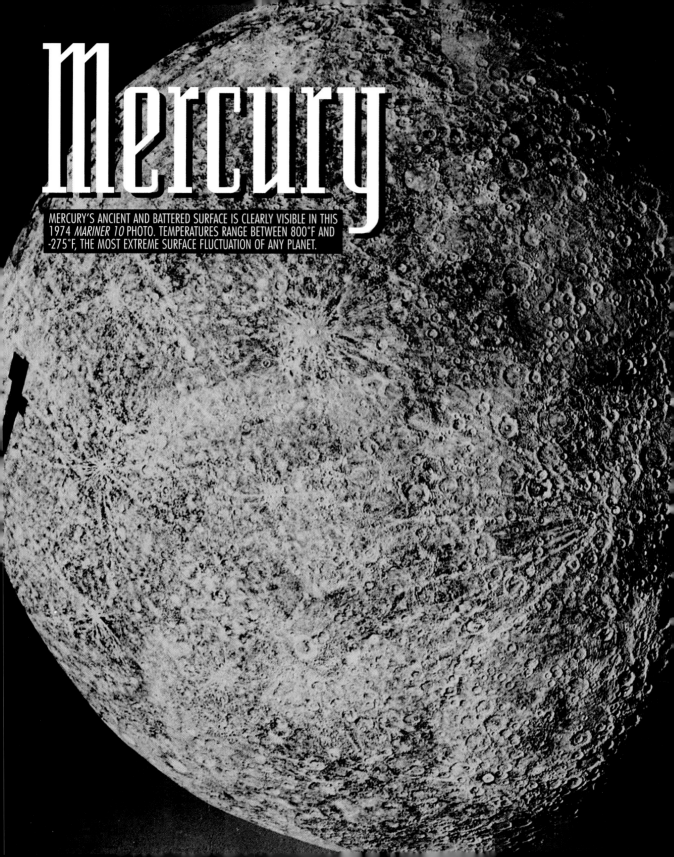

Mercury

MERCURY'S ANCIENT AND BATTERED SURFACE IS CLEARLY VISIBLE IN THIS
1974 *MARINER 10* PHOTO. TEMPERATURES RANGE BETWEEN 800°F AND
-275°F, THE MOST EXTREME SURFACE FLUCTUATION OF ANY PLANET.

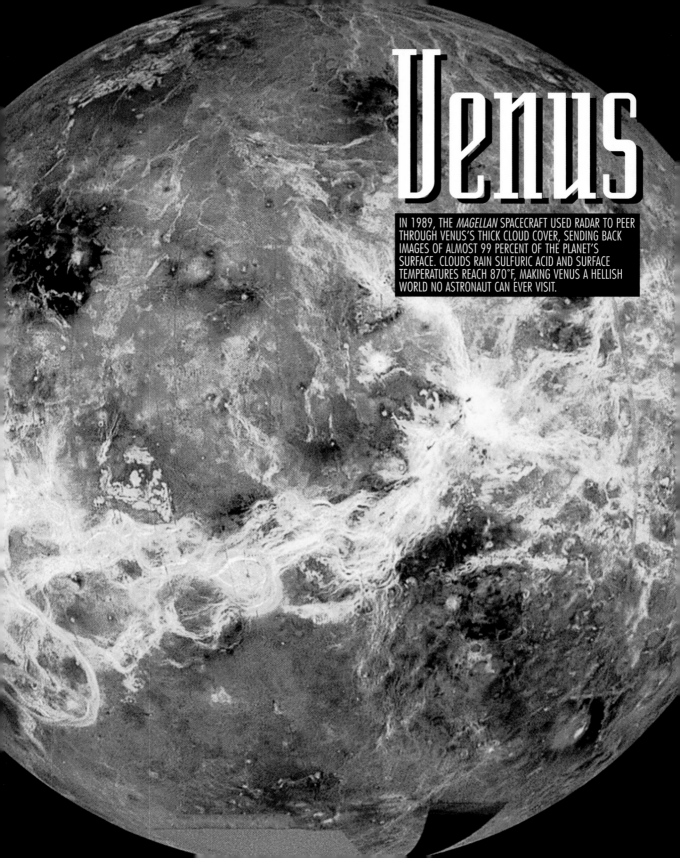

Venus

IN 1989, THE *MAGELLAN* SPACECRAFT USED RADAR TO PEER THROUGH VENUS'S THICK CLOUD COVER, SENDING BACK IMAGES OF ALMOST 99 PERCENT OF THE PLANET'S SURFACE. CLOUDS RAIN SULFURIC ACID AND SURFACE TEMPERATURES REACH 870°F, MAKING VENUS A HELLISH WORLD NO ASTRONAUT CAN EVER VISIT.

Earth

SO FAR AS WE KNOW, EARTH IS THE ONLY PLANET CAPABLE OF SUPPORTING LIFE—A PEACEFUL WORLD FLOATING IN A VIOLENT AND DEADLY UNIVERSE.

THE *MERCURY* PROGRAM BEGAN AMERICA'S MANNED SPACE PROGRAM. PICTURED ARE THE "MERCURY 7" ASTRONAUTS(LEFT TO RIGHT): FRONT ROW, W. SHIRRA, D. SLAYTON, J. GLENN, M.S. CARPENTER. BACK ROW, A. SHEPHARD, JR., V. GRISSOM, L.G. COOPER, JR.

GEMINI WAS THE SECOND PHASE OF THE U.S. MANNED SPACE PROGRAM. IT ALLOWED ASTRONAUTS TO PRACTICE MANY OF THE MANEUVERS REQUIRED TO FLY TO THE MOON WHILE ORBITING THE EARTH.

IN 1973, THE U.S. LAUNCHED *SKYLAB,* A TWO-STORY SPACE STATION FEATURING WORKSHOPS, LIVING QUARTERS AND A SOLAR TELESCOPE OBSERVATORY. *SKYLAB* ORBITED SIX YEARS BEFORE FALLING BACK TO EARTH AND BURNING UP IN THE ATMOSPHERE.

GETTING USED TO WEIGHTLESSNESS: *SKYLAB* ASTRONAUTS CONRAD AND KERWIN EXPERIMENTING IN ZERO-G

The Moon

EARTH'S MOON IS SOMETHING OF A MYSTERY—SO LARGE, COMPARED TO THE EARTH, THAT IT COULD REALLY BE CONSIDERED A DOUBLE PLANET INSTEAD OF A SATELLITE. SPACE SCIENTISTS ARE INVESTIGATING SEVERAL THEORIES ABOUT THE ORIGIN OF THIS ANCIENT, LIFELESS WORLD.

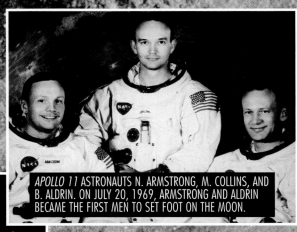

APOLLO 11 ASTRONAUTS N. ARMSTRONG, M. COLLINS, AND B. ALDRIN. ON JULY 20, 1969, ARMSTRONG AND ALDRIN BECAME THE FIRST MEN TO SET FOOT ON THE MOON.

APOLLO 15 ASTRONAUTS BROUGHT ALONG A LUNAR ROVING VEHICLE KNOWN AS "THE MOON BUGGY" (A MOON BUGGY WHEEL IS VISIBLE IN FRONT OF THE LANDER, LOWER RIGHT CORNER).

WILL ASTRONAUTS EVER RETURN TO THE MOON? *LUNAR PROSPECTOR,* LAUNCHED INTO LUNAR ORBIT IN 1998, IS GATHERING DATA THAT MAY PINPOINT THE BEST SPOT TO BUILD A FUTURE MOON COLONY.

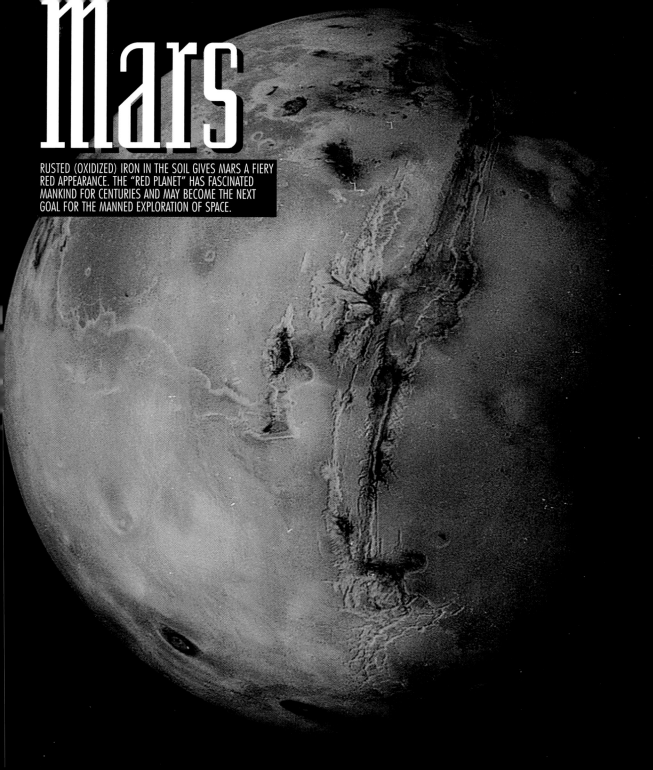

Mars

RUSTED (OXIDIZED) IRON IN THE SOIL GIVES MARS A FIERY RED APPEARANCE. THE "RED PLANET" HAS FASCINATED MANKIND FOR CENTURIES AND MAY BECOME THE NEXT GOAL FOR THE MANNED EXPLORATION OF SPACE.

PHOBOS, THE LARGER OF MARS'S TWO MOONS, ORBITS THE PLANET EVERY EIGHT HOURS. THIS *VIKING 1* PHOTO, TAKEN LESS THAN 400 MILES AWAY, FEATURES THE LARGE CRATER NAMED STICKNEY—THE RESULT OF AN IMPACT THAT NEARLY SHATTERED THE SMALL SATELLITE. RECENT DATA INDICATES METEORITE IMPACTS HAVE TURNED THE ENTIRE SURFACE OF PHOBOS INTO A FINE POWDER AT LEAST THREE FEET THICK!

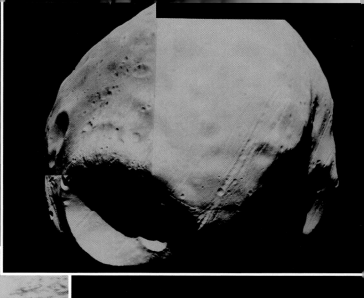

MARS BOASTS THE LARGEST VOLCANO OF ANY PLANET IN THE SOLAR SYSTEM: OLYMPUS MONS, TOWERING 15 MILES HIGH.

IN 1996, THE U.S. SENT AN UNMANNED PROBE NAMED *PATHFINDER* TO MARS, TO STUDY THE PLANET IN CLOSER DETAIL. AFTER LANDING, *PATHFINDER* RELEASED *SOJOURNER*, A SMALL, SIX-WHEELED ROBOT EXPLORER ABLE TO ROVE OVER THE MARTIAN LANDSCAPE AND ANALYZE THE SOIL, SEARCHING FOR MICROSCOPIC SIGNS OF LIFE. DATA REVEALED THAT IN THE DISTANT PAST, MARS WAS A WARMER, WETTER WORLD— PERHAPS EVEN SIMILAR TO EARTH.

Jupiter

JUPITER, KING OF THE PLANETS, IS A GAS GIANT SWIRLING WITH MULTICOLORED BANDS OF HYDROGEN, HELIUM, METHANE, AMMONIA, AND WATER VAPOR SURROUNDING A ROCKY CORE. WEST WINDS CAN REACH 100 MILES PER HOUR, AND EAST WINDS 270 MILES PER HOUR. WHERE THESE WINDS MEET, THEY CREATE STORMS THAT LAST FOR YEARS. ONE STORM, THE "GREAT RED SPOT," HAS RAGED FOR HUNDREDS OF YEARS, AND IS THREE TIMES THE SIZE OF THE EARTH!

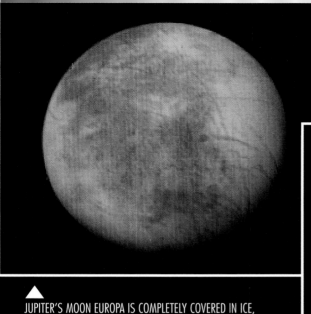

GANYMEDE IS THE LARGEST MOON IN THE SOLAR SYSTEM—BIGGER, IN FACT, THAN THE PLANET MERCURY! GANYMEDE HAS A MAGNETIC FIELD AND A THIN ATMOSPHERE OF ITS OWN, GIVING THE MOON SOME OF THE GEOLOGIC ACTIVITY COMMON TO LARGER, EARTHLIKE WORLDS.

▼

▲
JUPITER'S MOON EUROPA IS COMPLETELY COVERED IN ICE, MAKING IT THE SMOOTHEST SURFACE IN THE SOLAR SYSTEM. BENEATH THE ICE LIES A SUBTERRANEAN OCEAN, WHICH MAY BE HEATED BY UNDERSEA VENTS OR THE GRAVITATIONAL PULL OF JUPITER. SOME ASTRONOMERS BELIEVE EUROPA HAS THE NECESSARY INGREDIENTS TO CREATE LIFE.

CALLISTO, FURTHEST AWAY OF JUPITER'S FOUR LARGEST MOONS, IS AN ICE-COVERED WORLD POCKMARKED BY IMPACT CRATERS. LIKE GANYMEDE, IT IS LARGER THAN THE PLANET MERCURY.

▼

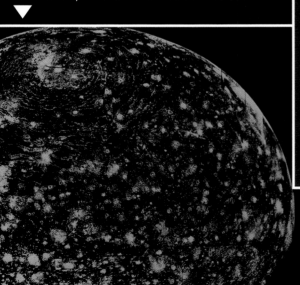

▲
STRANGEST OF ALL JUPITER'S MOONS MAY BE IO, THE MOST VOLCANICALLY-ACTIVE WORLD IN THE SOLAR SYSTEM. IO'S SURFACE IS CONSTANTLY BEING COVERED BY NEW ERUPTIONS, ERASING ALL TRACES OF METEOR IMPACTS. IN THIS *VOYAGER 1* PHOTO, A VOLCANIC PLUME CAN BE SEEN SPEWING HUNDREDS OF MILES INTO SPACE.

Saturn

SATURN IS THE MOST VISUALLY STUNNING OF OUR SOLAR SYSTEM'S FOUR RINGED PLANETS. LIKE JUPITER, IT IS A GAS GIANT, WITH A TURBULENT ATMOSPHERE WHERE STORMS CAN RAGE FOR YEARS. BUT IT IS SATURN'S REMARKABLE RINGS THAT HAVE DELIGHTED STARGAZERS AND FASCINATED ASTRONOMERS FOR CENTURIES.

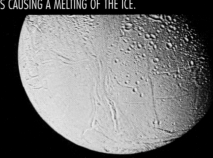

SATURN'S MOON ENCELADUS PRESENTS MYSTERIES: AN ICE-COVERED WORLD RIDDLED WITH IMPACT CRATERS, MANY SURFACE FEATURES HAVE BEEN ERASED—BUT HOW? ASTRONOMERS THEORIZE SOME UNKNOWN EVENT IS CAUSING A MELTING OF THE ICE.

SATURN'S RINGS, ORBITING PARTICLES OF ICE, ROCK, AND DUST, ARE VERY THIN—NO MORE THAN A HUNDRED YARDS WIDE. YET THEY STRETCH AS FAR AS 46,000 MILES INTO SPACE.

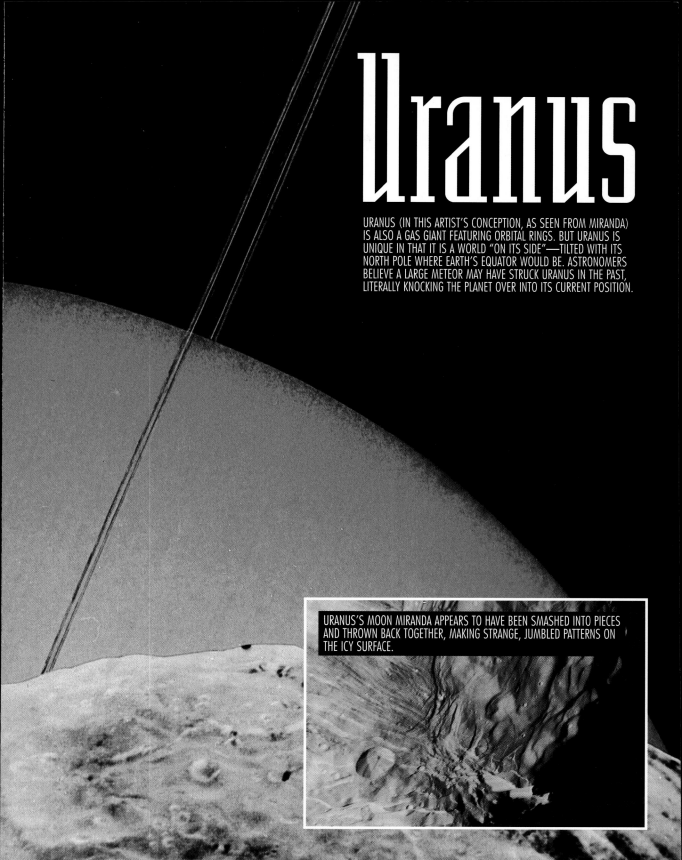

Uranus

URANUS (IN THIS ARTIST'S CONCEPTION, AS SEEN FROM MIRANDA) IS ALSO A GAS GIANT FEATURING ORBITAL RINGS. BUT URANUS IS UNIQUE IN THAT IT IS A WORLD "ON ITS SIDE"—TILTED WITH ITS NORTH POLE WHERE EARTH'S EQUATOR WOULD BE. ASTRONOMERS BELIEVE A LARGE METEOR MAY HAVE STRUCK URANUS IN THE PAST, LITERALLY KNOCKING THE PLANET OVER INTO ITS CURRENT POSITION.

URANUS'S MOON MIRANDA APPEARS TO HAVE BEEN SMASHED INTO PIECES AND THROWN BACK TOGETHER, MAKING STRANGE, JUMBLED PATTERNS ON THE ICY SURFACE.

Neptune

NEPTUNE IS THE LAST OF OUR SOLAR SYSTEM'S GAS GIANTS. LIKE THE OTHERS, IT HAS RAGING STORMS, INCLUDING ONE SYSTEM KNOWN AS THE "GREAT DARK SPOT," A CATACLYSM AS LARGE AS THE ENTIRE EARTH. NEPTUNE ALSO HAS FOUR ORBITING RINGS, ALTHOUGH THEY ARE FAINT AND INVISIBLE FROM A DISTANCE.

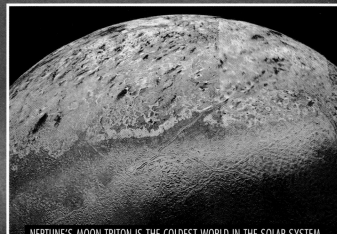

NEPTUNE'S MOON TRITON IS THE COLDEST WORLD IN THE SOLAR SYSTEM, WITH TEMPERATURES AS LOW AS -391°F.—SO COLD THAT VOLCANOS MAY SPEW FROZEN NITROGEN INSTEAD OF MOLTEN LAVA!

NOTE: PLUTO (NOT PICTURED) IS THE ONLY PLANET NOT YET PHOTOGRAPHED BY AN UNMANNED SPACE PROBE. (SEE PAGE 109)

Space Shuttle

THE SPACE SHUTTLE IS THE WORLD'S FIRST REUSABLE SPACECRAFT, DESIGNED TO FERRY ASTRONAUTS OR EQUIPMENT INTO EARTH ORBIT AND LAUNCH SATELLITES AND UNMANNED PROBES INTO SPACE.

EVEN THOUGH THE SHUTTLE LAUNCHES VERTICALLY, LIKE A ROCKET, IT LANDS HORIZONTALLY, GLIDING ONTO A RUNWAY LIKE AN ORDINARY AIRPLANE.

IN ORBIT, THE SHUTTLE'S CARGO BAY DOORS OPEN TO RELEASE EQUIPMENT, LAUNCH SPACE PROBES, OR PERFORM EXPERIMENTS IN ZERO-G.

Astronauts

THIS IS A GOLDEN AGE FOR SPACE EXPLORATION. TODAY, ASTRONAUTS MAINTAIN A CONTINUOUS PRESENCE IN EARTH ORBIT, AND MAY SOON RETURN TO THE MOON—OR EVEN MARS.

WITH THE REINSTATEMENT OF NASA'S "TEACHERS IN SPACE" PROGRAM, THE DAY MAY BE NEAR WHEN ORDINARY CITIZENS ARE ABLE TO FLY IN SPACE AT LAST!

THIRTY-FIVE YEARS AFTER BECOMING AMERICA'S FIRST ASTRONAUT TO ORBIT THE EARTH, JOHN GLENN—AT AGE SEVENTY-SEVEN—IS FLYING INTO SPACE AGAIN.

• A PRELAUNCH SMELL TEST •

No detail of spaceflight is too small to escape the notice—or noses—of NASA's mission planners. Before each shuttle takeoff, a team of dedicated volunteers at the White Sands Test Facility sniffs every odor-producing item intended for the flight, hoping to weed out anything that might make the astronauts scrunch up their noses in orbit. (Once an odor is aboard the shuttle, it has nowhere else to go!)

What sorts of things must pass the smell test? Odor-heavy items such as food, perfume, and deodorant are tested, of course, but so are everyday materials such as sleeping bag fabric and electrical components. All materials are sealed into a special chamber and heated to release fumes, then sniffed before being given the olfactory okay!

• DESIGNING MISSION PATCHES •

For an astronaut, every trip into space is special. To help commemorate each mission, flight crews are allowed to design their own "mission patch." Sometimes the astronauts draw their own patches, and sometimes they use designs offered by artists around the country. All mission patches are four inches wide and are sewn onto the suits worn during spaceflight. To view mission patches from the history of U.S. spaceflight, visit: http://www.hq.nasa.gov/office/pao/History/mission_patches.html

• PRECIOUS CARGO •

Whenever NASA launches a shuttle into orbit, it removes every spare ounce from the experiments and equipment on board. It costs almost $10,000 per pound to place cargo in low-Earth orbit!

Astronauts are allowed to carry no more than twenty personal items aboard the Space Shuttle. Typical items include Bibles, wedding rings, and good luck charms. NASA must approve all items before they are launched into orbit.

• LIVING IN SPACE •

Space is a dangerous environment, hotter and drier than an African desert and colder than a winter storm at the South Pole. How can it be both hot and cold? In space, the temperature near Earth varies, depending on whether you are in direct sunlight or in shadow. Space-walking astronauts floating in the shadow of the shuttle would find themselves in a frigid -250°F, but if they should float into the sunlight the temperature could soar as high as 250°F!

An astronaut must rely completely on his or her equipment for survival. An astronaut's space suit offers protection from the airless vacuum of space and also acts as a shield against extremes of heat and cold.

• WHAT DO ASTRONAUTS EAT? •

In the early days of the space program, providing astronauts with delicious meals was a low priority. Most food was liquefied and squeezed out of tubes, and nothing tasted very good. Today's shuttle astronauts eat food not too different from what we eat on Earth. Even better, each astronaut can sample the available menu and choose his or her own favorite meals before lift-off!

Space Shuttle astronauts are able to select their meals from a wide range of available foods. A typical day's menu might include:

EATING IN SPACE CAN BE A TRICKY EXPERIENCE ▲

Breakfast

strawberries

oatmeal with brown sugar

granola with raisins

granola bar

breakfast roll

orange juice

coffee with cream and sugar

Lunch

shrimp cocktail

spaghetti with meat sauce

green beans with mushrooms

tapioca pudding

brownie

lemonade

Dinner

shrimp cocktail

smoked turkey

noodles and chicken

green beans and broccoli

peach ambrosia

lemonade

• SNACKING IN SPACE •

Spacewalking outside the shuttle is a complex activity. It can take several hours to complete an extravehicular activity (EVA). What if an astronaut gets hungry or thirsty? In the past, spacewalkers had to wait until they returned to their capsules to eat or drink. Now, NASA has developed a way for astronauts to snack from inside their spacesuits: An energy bar and water pouch are attached to the interior of each suit, just below the helmet. All a hungry spacewalker needs to do is tilt his or her head downward to enjoy a snack in space!

• A BALL OF WATER, PLEASE •

Among other things, space is one place where you needn't worry about spilling a drink. Why not? When liquid is released in zero gravity, the floating molecules all pull at one another, forming a perfect sphere—a ball of liquid floating in the air!

• THE QUESTION PEOPLE ASK MOST •

One of the most frequently asked questions about living in space is "How do astronauts go to the bathroom?" The answer is: "Just like we do at home." The Space Shuttle's toilet is designed to match Earth toilets as closely as possible. It flushes with jets of air instead of water, and it uses filters to remove odors and bacteria. The same toilet is used by all astronauts aboard the shuttle.

• TAKING OUT THE TRASH •

Outer space is littered with the remains of decades of human exploration. Aboard the limited space of the *Mir* space station, however, trash piles up. Since the U.S. Space Shuttle visits *Mir* regularly, unloading trash onto the shuttle is the cheapest way to return the excess cargo to Earth. U.S. astronauts have been recruited as garbage collectors on special missions designed to remove rubbish from the eleven-year-old space station.

Not all junk in space is left over from important scientific missions. Among the garbage returned to Earth over the years were empty food containers, tainted water, broken radio components, and even an old guitar. During *Apollo 15*, in August 1971, a crew member's toothbrush and comb floated through an open hatchway during a space walk and began their own orbit of the Earth.

Are they still up there? Nope! Just two days later, Earth's gravity pulled them into the atmosphere, where they burned up like tiny meteors. Most of the trash left in low-Earth orbit will eventually burn up in the atmosphere. Some trash, however, is small and light enough to remain in orbit for hundreds of years.

NASA is exploring ways to reduce the trash left behind on future space missions. One plan proposes using high-powered lasers to pinpoint individual pieces of debris and disturb their orbits just enough to pull them downward into Earth's fiery atmosphere—and certain destruction. Other, less daring plans envision sending special shuttles skyward to collect large amounts of debris and return the rubbish safely to the ground.

• PHONING HOME •

Scientists have learned that astronauts work better on space missions if they feel connected to the Earth. In addition to daily communication with Mission Control, astronauts on long missions (ten days or more) are allowed one fifteen-minute private call with their families. Since there are no telephone wires in space, the call is made via two-way radio.

Radio isn't the only way orbiting astronauts can communicate with Earth, however; the shuttle can receive faxes and e-mail, too. All messages are currently relayed through Mission Control, but one day you may be able to send an e-mail directly to the shuttle or the International Space Station yourself!

• SURF THE INTERNET TO THE MOON •

Today, it's common to log on to the Internet and "surf" to Web sites all over the world, but

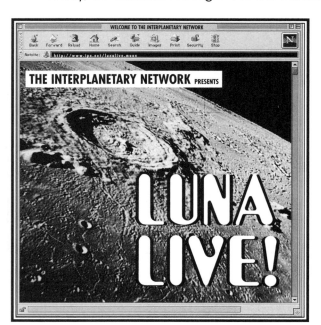

NASA envisions expanding the Internet into an interplanetary web connecting Earth with the rest of the solar system! The Interplanetary Network (IPN) would combine today's Internet technology with satellite relays and other deep-space communications to allow information and messages to flow between the Earth, the Moon, and the other planets.

In the beginning, NASA plans to use such a system to communicate with unmanned probes it sends into space. In the future, however, Internet browsers could log on and surf their way to Web sites and e-mail addresses that end with ".moon" or ".saturn" instead of ".com" (company) or ".org" (organization).

• SEE THE SHUTTLE PASS OVERHEAD! •

The *Sky & Telescope* Web site generates a naked-eye visibility chart, listing where and when you can see the shuttle orbiting overhead for a hundred selected North American cities and a hundred other cities around the globe. This chart is updated with each new shuttle mission. The web address is: http://www.skypub.com/shuttle/shuttle.html

For a list of shuttle mission numbers, visit: http://www.hq.nasa.gov/osf/shuttle/futsts.html

It's also possible to see *Mir* pass overhead as it orbits the Earth. A naked eye visibility chart for *Mir* can be found at: http://www.hq.nasa.gov/osf/mir/mirvis.html

SPACE QUIZ

Q: What's the record for the most astronauts in space at one time?

A: Twelve. During the week of December 2, 1990, five cosmonauts aboard *Soyuz TM-11* and seven astronauts aboard the shuttle *Columbia* orbited the Earth on separate missions.

THE SHUTTLE IN ORBIT

The longest the Space Shuttle can safely remain in Earth orbit is 16 days. Shuttles have no renewable energy source and are designed with a two-week supply of electricity (which can be stretched for two extra days, if necessary).

Space Stations

A space station is an orbiting spacecraft designed to house astronauts for long periods of time. In 1971, the Soviet Union (now Russia) launched the world's first space station, *Salyut 1.* It was a fairly simple tube-shaped craft, 47 feet long and 13 feet wide, with four solar panels providing electrical power.

After six months, *Salyut 1* fell into Earth's atmosphere and was destroyed. Over the next twenty years, the Soviets launched six more *Salyut* stations. During that time, cosmonauts performed thousands of experiments on missions lasting as long as 237 days. Space stations have taught scientists a lot about what it takes for humans to survive in zero gravity.

• A STATION CALLED *SKYLAB* •

In 1973, the United States launched a space station called *Skylab*. It orbited the Earth for six years, staffed by astronauts arriving and departing in *Apollo* capsules. A wide range of scientific experiments were performed onboard. Eventually, however, *Skylab*'s orbit decayed. The station tumbled into Earth's atmosphere, where it disintegrated, raining debris across the Indian Ocean and Australia.

SKYLAB IN ORBIT ▲

• MUTINY IN SPACE •

Skylab's third crew set an endurance record for American astronauts, by orbiting the Earth for eighty-four days. Researchers were very interested in learning about the long-term effects of living in space, and they assigned the astronauts long lists of experiments to perform in the weightless environment.

What scientists learned, however, was that living in space is difficult work and that astronauts, just like people on Earth, need time to relax and play. Tired and pressured by ground controllers to do too many chores, the *Skylab* astronauts refused to continue working until a new schedule allowed them more time to rest.

Their mutiny changed the way America's space missions are planned. Today's shuttle astronauts are given time to rest, play games, take pictures, and simply enjoy their view of the stars. Life in space has become a lot more fun.

• A STATION CALLED "PEACE" •

Russia's *Mir* has been orbiting the Earth for twelve years, longer than any other space station. Its name comes from the Russian word for "peace"—and *Mir* has been a model of peaceful cooperation in space.

Mir consists of six laboratory modules, launched separately and joined together in orbit. An extra module added in 1995 allows U.S. shuttles to dock at the station.

THE *MIR* SPACE STATION ▲

PROJECT GREENHOUSE

NASA astronauts and Russian cosmonauts, working together on *Mir*, have succeeded in harvesting the first crop ever grown in zero gravity. Their experiment, conducted with a breed of "super-dwarf" wheat, represents the first time plants have survived an entire life cycle in space. Growing food in space is an important breakthrough. Self-sustaining space stations must be able to replenish their food supplies, and the same techniques will one day be used to grow food on other worlds for manned space colonies.

Though astronauts from many different countries have been guests aboard *Mir,* Americans have been permanent residents since March 1996. NASA astronauts Norman Thagard, Shannon Lucid, John Blaha, Jerry Linenger, Michael Foale, David Wolf, and Andy Thomas have all spent time aboard the Russian space station.

RUSSIAN RECORDS IN SPACE

Cosmonaut Valeri Polyakov holds the current record for the longest period in orbit, spending 438 days aboard the *Mir* space station. The record for the most space walks is held by cosmonaut Anatoly Solovyov—sixteen EVAs, (extravehicular activities) totaling more than seventy hours floating freely in space.

• A SPACE PLACE WITHOUT A NAME •

In 1984, U.S. President Ronald Reagan announced plans for a new orbital space station called *Freedom.* When Congress decided the project was too expensive, the United States looked to other countries to help share costs. Russia, Europe, Canada, and Japan soon joined the effort, turning the station into an international space project.

Many years later, the first components are ready to be blasted into orbit, beginning a five-year space construction effort requiring forty-five separate launches. The completed station will be 361 feet across and 290 feet long and weigh almost 100,000 pounds. Beginning in 1999, six astronauts will live on board full-time.

Yet the new space station remains without a name. In Russia, the station is called *Alpha* (the first letter of the Greek alphabet). NASA calls the project The *International Space Station (ISS).* But most space projects usually have a shorter name, something everyday citizens can remember without any trouble.

THE *INTERNATIONAL SPACE STATION* ▲

America's Space Shuttles are named after famous sailing ships: *Columbia, Challenger, Discovery, Atlantis,* and *Endeavour.* Most space probes are named after famous scientists or explorers.

At some point over the next five years, the space station participants will have to agree on the project's final name. If you have an idea for a name, you can write it down and send it to NASA at:

Johnson Space Center
Information Services
Code AP4
Houston, TX 77058

You never know what might happen: Thousands of *Star Trek* fans wrote to NASA at the beginning of the Space Shuttle program, asking that the first shuttle be named *Enterprise.* NASA agreed, and the first shuttle flown—a test vehicle—was named after the famous television starship.

MANNED SPACE STATIONS

1971	*Salyut 1*	USSR
1973–79	*Skylab*	USA
1974–82	*Salyut 3, 4, 5, 6*	USSR
1983–present	*Spacelab* (in Shuttle bay)	USA & ESA
1982–86	*Salyut 7*	USSR
1986–present	*Mir*	USSR
manned in 1999	*International Space Station*	International

• AN EMERGENCY TRIP HOME •

If something goes wrong with their equipment, astronauts need a quick way to return home without waiting for a rescue vehicle to be launched from Earth. NASA has placed an escape hatch in the crew compartment of the shuttle so that astronauts can leave the ship in an emergency. Russia's *Mir* space station always has a *Soyuz* space capsule attached to be used by cosmonauts in the event of a disaster. And the new International Space Station, when it is completed, will also have a *Soyuz* escape pod attached for emergencies in case a Space Shuttle is not readily available.

The *Soyuz* capsule, however, can carry just three passengers. At some point in the future, a more advanced and specialized vehicle must be available for emergency situations that require the entire space station crew's evacuation. NASA is currently testing an experimental craft called the X-38, designed to carry seven passengers from space to Earth. If successful, the X-38 could become a permanent rescue pod attached to the International Space Station.

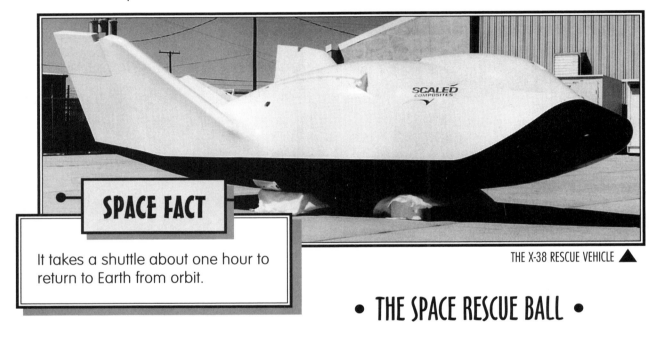

SPACE FACT

It takes a shuttle about one hour to return to Earth from orbit.

THE X-38 RESCUE VEHICLE ▲

• THE SPACE RESCUE BALL •

The Space Shuttle carries a crew of seven, but because only a few mission specialists venture outside the capsule, only three space suits are stored on board. What happens if the entire crew has to abandon ship? Each astronaut climbs into a space rescue ball. Rescue balls are made from the same stuff as space suits, and protect astronauts from extreme heat and cold. An onboard oxygen supply can keep occupants alive for several hours (hopefully, until another rescue vehicle arrives).

In the event of a sudden space disaster, rescue teams could arrive to find seven little balls orbiting the Earth, each carrying precious human cargo inside!

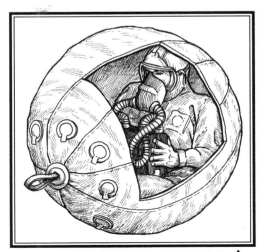

THE SPACE RESCUE BALL: A LIFEBOAT IN SPACE ▲

Space and the Future

Humankind has stared at the heavens for thousands of years, but we have been exploring space for only a fraction of that time. Our future will take us farther and faster into space than ever before, to explore places that were once the stuff of dreams.

• THE SPACE PLANE •

The Space Shuttle is the world's first reusable spacecraft, but in order to achieve escape velocity it requires large external fuel tanks (which are cast off into the sea after launch). For years, rocket engineers have dreamed of a reusable spacecraft that could launch into space by itself and return from space to land like an airplane. Now that dream may become a reality at last.

In 1999, America will begin its first full-size tests of the X-33 rocket, also known as the "space plane" or "lifting body." The X-33 (which looks a little bit like a shorter, fatter Space Shuttle) is designed to take off without external fuel tanks and land on ordinary airport runways. If all goes as planned, traveling into space may soon become as simple as flying to the next city. For more information on the X-33, visit: http://vab02.larc.nasa.gov/Activities/X-33.html

THE NEXT GENERATION OF FLYING OBSERVATORY

NASA is making plans for its next generation of flying observatory to replace the aging Kuiper Airborne Observatory. When it is launched, the Stratospheric Observatory for Infrared Astronomy (SOFIA) will carry a 100-inch lens in a converted Boeing 747 jet. (The Kuiper has a 36-inch lens.) Scientists hope to complete the project and have SOFIA flying by the year 2000. For more information on SOFIA, visit: http://sofia.arc.nasa.gov

• CAPTURING COMETS •

Early in 1999, NASA plans to launch a spacecraft called *Stardust* on an exciting five-year journey to rendezvous with comet Wild-2, some 242 million miles from Earth. If all goes well, *Stardust* will become the first spacecraft to collect samples of a comet and return them to Earth.

Capturing pieces of a comet is a difficult task. Even the smallest particles hurl through space at incredible speeds. (Wild-2 travels at 14,000 miles per hour, six times faster than a speeding bullet!) To collect samples safely and return them to Earth, scientists are using a new substance called "aerogel." Aerogel is the lightest man-made substance in the world. Made of silica (sand), 99 percent of its volume is made up of empty space—so much empty space, in fact, that aerogel is often called "blue smoke." Yet aerogel is very strong, and comet particles that strike it will bury themselves inside, becoming trapped in a protective cocoon for the long homeward journey.

Astronomer Paul Wild, the astronomer who discovered the comet (and for whom Wild-2 is named), has encoded a personal message onto a microchip that will accompany *Stardust* on its long journey:

"If my life span is more than eighty years, I would greatly like to witness the happy return of the precious dust and to inspect at close range a wee bit of what I first spied from very far."

For more information on the *Stardust* mission, visit: http://stardust.jpl.nasa.gov

• A TRIP TO THE BEGINNING OF TIME •

Astronomers often refer to comets as "orphans" left over from the birth of the solar system, since all other material gathered together to form the Sun, the planets, and their moons. Some scientists believe comets are made up of material that could show how life began in the universe.

NASA has devised an ambitious new project called the *Deep Space-4 Champollion* mission, scheduled for launch in April 2003. *Deep Space 4* will fly to the comet Tempel 1, which orbits the Sun every five and a half years. After traveling hundreds of millions of miles into space, the probe will rendezvous with the comet, throw out a harpoon, and detach the *Champollion* lander for descent to its surface. It will then drill into the comet's core and return samples to Earth for closer study.

The spacecraft's lander is named after Jean François Champollion (1790–1832), who was not an astronomer but rather a scholar who unlocked the meaning of Egyptian hieroglyphics and first translated the mysterious pictographic writing for the modern world. Because

Deep Space 4 is a mission to explore—bodies that may unlock mysteries about the origin and evolution of the planets—the lander was named in his honor.

Nothing like this has ever been tried before in the history of space exploration. *Deep Space 4* is part of NASA's New Millennium Program, intended to develop and test new technologies. The spacecraft should complete its dramatic journey by June 2010. For more information on *Deep Space 4*, visit: http://nmp.jpl.nasa.gov

• THE *PLUTO EXPRESS* •

Pluto is the only planet in our solar system not yet visited by robotic probes. If all goes as planned, however, a new spacecraft, the *Pluto Express*, will arrive at our most distant planet in 2013 and begin relaying pictures back to Earth.

Because it has to travel more than three and a half billion miles, the *Pluto Express* can't rely on solar panels for power. Instead, it will have a small amount of nuclear fuel on board, enough to last the probe for its twelve-year journey.

The spacecraft is named *Express* because it will travel to the far planet as quickly as possible. When Pluto is far from the Sun, the coldness of space turns it into a frozen ball of ice; but in 2013 Pluto will be at its closest to the Sun (the perihelion). The Sun's heat will melt Pluto's icy exterior, creating an atmosphere astronomers are eager to explore. If a spacecraft doesn't visit Pluto during its perihelion, in 2013, we will have to wait 250 years before the next opportunity arrives. For more information on the *Pluto Express* mission, visit: http://www.jpl.nasa.gov/pluto

• COLLECTING THE SOLAR WIND •

People think of space as an airless vacuum, but in fact it's a windy place. The Sun is always putting out charged particles that stream through space. NASA has devised a mission to collect samples of this solar wind and return them to Earth for closer examination. Astronomers hope that studying the very particles that formed the planets (isotopes of oxygen, nitrogen, and other elements) will help them learn more about the birth of our solar system and its probable future.

The mission, dubbed *Genesis*, is part of the "new generation" of NASA spacecraft designed to be smaller, faster, and cheaper. Instead of carrying several scientific instruments, *Genesis* will be equipped for a specific purpose. The mission, scheduled for launch in January 2001, should return its samples to Earth by 2003. For more information on the *Genesis* mission, visit: http://nssdc.gsfc.nasa.gov/cgi-bin/database/www-nmc?GENESIS

• GUIDING BY THE STARS •

Throughout most of human history, sailors have navigated the seas by charting constellations in the sky—using stars to plot their progress. In the future, when explorers sail through the vast reaches of space, they may again come to rely on the stars to help guide their way.

Astronomers have discovered a special kind of star called a *pulsar* (so called because it pulses with radiation at regular intervals). No two pulsars are exactly alike. By identifying and cataloging each pulsating star and its radiation "fingerprint," space travelers of the future will be able to map their time and progress through space with absolute precision.

SPACE JARGON

Pulsar: The tiny core of a dead star, spinning rapidly in space. Pulsars emit radio waves in regular pulses, creating a flashing light beacon.

A FLEET OF • TINY SPACESHIPS •

In the past, NASA's spaceships have been large, heavy machines, weighing as much as six tons each. In order to escape Earth's gravity, they had to be launched into space by gigantic multistage rockets delivering thousands of pounds of vertical thrust. What's more, they were very expensive to build. Each time a probe malfunctioned, millions of dollars were lost.

The future of space exploration, however, may rely on fleets of tiny spaceships that can be launched like swarms of tiny insects. As part of NASA's new policy to build "faster, smarter, cheaper" spacecraft, engineers are designing a new breed of probes no bigger than a few inches wide!

Despite their small size, these microprobes are intelligent craft. They have control systems that mimic circuits in the human brain. Early tests have produced tiny, walking robots able to think for themselves and survive electrical disturbances (such as might be produced by a solar flare in space).

An entire swarm of these spacecraft could function together like a single vessel or scatter to perform separate tasks. Not only might this ability provide much more data from future space missions (since multiple machines can land across a wide portion of a planet instead of at a single site), but it would allow the larger mission to continue unaffected if any single component failed.

• SPACE COLONIES •

Ever since the earliest science fiction stories, humans have dreamed of living on other worlds. At first, before planetary atmospheres were understood, it was assumed that people could breathe on Mars and Venus, and possibly even on the Moon. Gradually, as telescopes improved and space probes traveled to other worlds, scientists leaned that space was a cold, airless place where no human could survive without the protection of an artificial environment.

The first artificial environments were space suits and space capsules. Space stations are larger versions of the same idea. But for humans to live and work in space in large numbers, a new technology will have to be perfected: self-sustaining artificial habitats (better known as "space colonies").

Why create space colonies? For one thing, developing artificial, self-sustaining habitats may create technologies that will help preserve life on Earth. More important, if Earth were ever threatened by an asteroid or other global disaster, space colonies might give the human race its best chance to begin again . . . on another world.

• BIOSPHERE 2 •

In 1991, four men and four women entered a glass building in the Arizona desert, promising not to leave for two years, when a new team of scientists would enter to replace them. Rotating eight-person crews would then live and work in the same building for the next hundred years.

Such was the dream of a gigantic complex called *Biosphere 2*, billed as the world's largest self-sustaining environment. ("Biosphere 1" is the Earth itself.) *Biosphere 2* was designed as a test facility for space colonies—a place to learn about surviving without the outside world. Inside the habitat's three acres of buildings are ocean, desert, farm, marsh, and jungle environments and nearly 4,000 different types of plants and animals. All of the air, water, and waste inside the facility is recycled without outside maintenance.

Unfortunately, the technologies required to maintain large artificial habitats have not yet been perfected, and two years after the project began the original *Biosphere 2* project was ended. Today, the facility has been transformed into a university laboratory rather than a sealed ecosphere. But if humans are ever to build permanent colonies on the Moon, on Mars, or elsewhere in the galaxy, we must first learn how to survive without materials or help from Earth. With experiments like *Biosphere 2*, humankind's future settlement of space has already begun. For more information on the *Biosphere 2* Center, visit: http://www.bio2.edu

• TERRAFORMING MARS •

The second most likely site for a manned space colony is Mars, a planet that may have been very similar to Earth in the distant past. Mars is near enough to the Sun to offer warmth and solar energy. (The temperature can reach 72°F.) Polar ice caps hold vast amounts of available water. The Martian atmosphere is rich in carbon dioxide, which plants breathe and convert to oxygen. At first, frequent supply ships from Earth would be required to supplement the available raw materials, but eventually a self-sustaining Martian colony could be created.

The basic ingredients might exist, in fact, to "terraform" the entire planet, creating a self-sustaining, breathable atmosphere. How long might that take? Experts estimate that humans could begin terraforming Mars within a century if they wanted to.

DESIGN EARTH'S FIRST ORBITAL SPACE COLONY FOR NASA!

Have you ever dreamed of designing an actual space colony? Now you can, thanks to NASA's annual Ames Research Center contest! Each year, students ages eleven to eighteen are invited to submit to NASA their best ideas for orbiting space settlements. The winning contestants are invited to work with NASA designers and display their submissions on an official Web site.
For more information, write to:

Al Globus, MS T27A-1
NASA Ames Research Center
Moffett Field, CA 94035

or visit the contest Web site at:
http://science.nas.nasa.gov/Services/Education/SpaceSettlement/Contest

• TAKE YOUR NEXT HOLIDAY IN SPACE? •

For decades, science fiction writers have dreamed of a future where ordinary people could travel into space to visit exotic, off-world colonies. Now, it seems, some of those far-flung dreams may soon be coming true.

In October 1997, the World Tourism Organization (WTO) issued a report on vacation trends and expectations for the future. The report predicted that by 2020 global tourism will have doubled from present levels, and people will be looking for places to travel that no one has ever visited before. This trend will be the beginning of "space tourism," an industry that can expect to grow quickly as we move further into the twenty-first century.

• BEAM ME UP, NASA •

For generations of TV watchers, "beaming up" is as familiar a way to get from one place to another as riding an elevator. Who hasn't wished they could be "transported" instantly across space? Now, it seems, science may make teleportation a reality at last.

Working in an Austrian laboratory, physicists have developed a technique to send photons of light across short distances and reassemble them perfectly. The process, called "quantum teleportation," relies on an unusual characteristic of light: Unlike other elementary matter, photons of light function as both particles and waves, seemingly "communicating" across invisible space (an aspect of physics that Einstein called "spooky"). What affects light particles in one area can determine the outcome of matched particles elsewhere, even in a separate room! (Why this is so, no one is certain.)

Making use of this characteristic, physicists are able to break down photons of light and reassemble them elsewhere. Of course, that's a long way from transporting entire human beings, but researchers predict that their initial experiments will soon extend from photons to atoms, and then to whole molecules. The day may yet arrive when "beaming up" is the favorite way to travel!

• THE DEATH OF OUR SUN •

Although our Sun is only halfway through its ten-billion-year life span, astronomers can predict how it will one day die. After burning up all its hydrogen fuel, only the lighter gas helium will remain. At this point, the Sun will become a red giant, growing in size until it consumes the inner planets—Mercury, Venus, Earth, and Mars. Some of the outer planets, receiving extra warmth and light from the now gigantic Sun, may develop climates hospitable to life.

Eventually, all the Sun's outer layers of gas will escape into space, leaving a small core called a white dwarf, and the rest of the solar system will grow cold and die. As the Sun's core cools, it will become a dark lifeless sphere floating in space—a black dwarf.

• THE BIG CRUNCH •

Scientists believe our universe began as an infinitely small point in space called a "singularity," which exploded into everything we know today (an event called the "Big Bang").

But what about the future? Will our universe keep expanding forever, growing colder in the icy world of space? Probably not. One theory suggests that the universe will stop expanding one day and begin to collapse, eventually returning to a single point in space. Astronomers call this collapse the "Big Crunch."

What would life be like in a collapsing universe? No one knows for certain, but it's possible that time will move in reverse. And when the Big Crunch becomes a singularity, a new universe might be born in a second Big Bang.

• THE PLATEAU THEORY •

Another prediction for the fate of the universe is often called the "Plateau Theory." According to this calculation, our universe will slowly stop expanding and eventually "freeze" in place.

• THE STEADY-STATE THEORY •

The "Steady-State Theory" suggests that the universe has always been the same as it appears today and will continue to be the same in the distant future. This theory holds that no matter which galaxy or star you might travel to, the view would be essentially the same.

• THE BIG CHILL •

Another theory (supported by some observational data) about the possible fate of our universe is called the "Big Chill." It proposes that the universe will continue to expand forever, making galaxies move farther and farther apart. Over time, as stars died, distances between galaxies would grow so great that space would eventually become cold and dark, a lonely and lifeless place.

FURTHER EXPLORATION

This is a golden age for space exploration. With astronauts maintaining a continuous presence in Earth orbit, unmanned probes reaching to the edge of the solar system, and telescopes able to peer back to the very beginning of the universe, we are learning more than ever before. There are many ways that everybody can get involved in space exploration. Here are a list of space-related books, CD-ROMs, films, videos, and Web sites to explore.

• KIDS IN SPACE •

Do you want to become an astronomer or program part of a Space Shuttle mission? Now you can, and you don't even have to wait until college thanks to a revolutionary program called KidSat.

KidSat is a NASA project designed for kids. It links students in schools across the United States to a still camera mounted aboard the Space Shuttle, allowing them to receive digital images of the Earth from space. Students must plan their photos carefully, calculating the coordinates of an area they'd like to photograph and the exact time the shuttle will be orbiting overhead. A computer relays this information to the shuttle, and the pictures are taken automatically. Another computer on board the shuttle then sends the pictures back to Earth, where they appear on computer screens in the classroom.

Begun in March 1996, KidSat has flown on three shuttle missions, and more flights are planned for the future. Some of the subjects studied so far include Earth's weather patterns, the flow of rivers, and a search for impact craters created by asteroids. To learn more about KidSat and to see some of the pictures taken thus far, visit: http://kidsat.jpl.nasa.gov

• CAN I WRITE TO AN ASTRONAUT? •

Can you write to a real astronaut and get a personal response? The answer, surprisingly, is yes! Here are the mailing addresses of some of America's most famous space pioneers. Be sure to enclose a self-addressed, stamped envelope to receive a personal reply.

First man on the Moon	Neil A. Armstrong P.O. Box 436 Lebanon, OH 45036
Second man on the Moon	Dr. Buzz Aldrin Starcraft Enterprise 233 Emerald Bay Laguna Beach, CA 92651
Commander of *Apollo 13*	James A. Lovell President Lovell Communications P.O. Box 49 Lake Forest, IL 60045
First female U.S. astronaut	Dr. Sally K. Ride Director California Space Institute University of California at San Diego La Jolla, CA 92093
First African-American woman in space	Dr. Mae Jemison The Jemison Group P.O. Box 591455 Houston, TX 77259-1455

• HOW DO I BECOME AN ASTRONAUT FOR A DAY? •

Even if you don't qualify to join NASA's astronaut training program, you can still experience what it's like to be a space person—at the U.S. Space Camp, Space Academy, and Aviation Challenge. These private programs are available to children, adults, and teachers, with sessions scheduled in Alabama and Florida. For more information, contact:

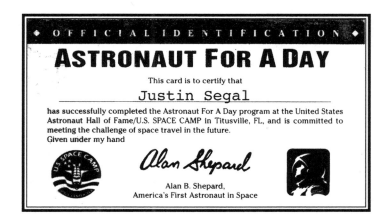

U.S. Space Camp, Space Academy & Aviation Challenge
U.S. Space & Rocket Center
One Tranquility Base
Huntsville, Alabama 35807

1-800-63-SPACE or (205) 837-3400

HOW CAN I JOIN THE SPACE PROGRAM WITHOUT BECOMING AN ASTRONAUT?

It takes all kinds of special people to make America's space program succeed. NASA has over 20,000 employees, and a limited number of internships (training positions) are available. For more information, write to:

Office of Human Resources and Education
Mail Code F
NASA Headquarters
300 E. St. SW
Washington, D.C. 20546

Or visit NASA's Public Affairs Office Web site at: http://www.nasa.gov/hqpao/ hqpao_home.html

• YOU, TOO, CAN BE A NASA ASTRONOMER •

There's more to amateur astronomy than enjoying the stars through a backyard tele- scope. Believe it or not, NASA considers amateur astronomers an important part of its space-watching missions. You can contact NASA and become an official observer!

Forty amateur astronomers participated during the *Clementine* orbiter mission to the Moon. Many more will be needed during the *Lunar Prospector* mission. For more information, contact:

David Darling
Coordinator
Transient Phenomena for the Association of Lunar and Planetary Observers (ALPO)
416 W. Wilson St.
Sun Prairie, WI 53590-2114

Or e-mail messages to:
DOD121252@aol.com

• SPACE WEB SITES* •

The Internet is a fantastic place to explore the wonders of space. Thousands of Web sites are devoted to individual missions, planets, astronomical phenomena, and countless other celestial happenings.

National Aeronautics and Space Administration
http://www.nasa.gov
NASA's official Web site, with daily updates, downloads, links to active missions, news, and information on future projects. A must-see for any space enthusiast.

Jet Propulsion Laboratory
http://www.jpl.nasa.gov
The Jet Propulsion Laboratory (JPL) designs and manages America's interplanetary space-craft. An excellent site for up-to-date information on planets, spacecraft, and other news about the universe.

Space Team Online
http://quest.arc.nasa.gov/shuttle
A site devoted to the men and women who make the Space Shuttle fly, including team information, field journals, photos, and a chance to pose questions to NASA experts.

Smithsonian's National Air and Space Museum
http://www.nasm.edu
The Smithsonian Institution is often called "America's attic," and the National Air and Space Museum is filled with exhibits from the history of flight and space exploration.

The Planetary Society
http://www.planetary.org
The official site of the Planetary Society, with information about membership, space, the planets, hot topics, a young explorers' program, and more.

Mission Control
http://www.personal.vineyard.net/jamie/msnctrl.htm
A good overall site for links to the latest space news, manned space flight, unmanned probes, astronomy, NASA space centers, and more.

The International Meteor Organization
http://www.imo.net
An organization dedicated to amateur meteor observation and discovery.

Ask a NASA Scientist!

http://imagine.gsfc.nasa.gov/docs/ask_astro/ask_an_astronomer.html

A great compendium of facts about all the mysteries of the universe. If you can't find it here, ask a NASA scientist and receive a personal reply!

Ask a Rocket Scientist

http://www.labs.net/rocket/ask/ask.htm

Do you dream of designing spaceships? Of voyaging to the stars? Have you ever wished for a chance to talk to a real rocket scientist? "Ask me anything!" is this site's motto.

SKY Online

http://www.skypub.com

Sign up for a wide spectrum of astronomy mailing lists.

*All Web sites listed were active at date of publication.

• SPECIAL KIDS' SITES •

Kid's Space

http://liftoff.msfc.nasa.gov/kids/welcome.html

A great place to explore space, including such features as "Kid's Quiz," "Word Find Puzzles," "Space Cadet Academy," "Zero Gravity," and "Unscramble Spacey Pictures." Fun for all ages.

Space Team Online: Kid's Corner

http://quest.arc.nasa.gov/shuttle/kids/index.html

A junior section of the Space Team Online site, with a gallery of student stories, poems, artwork, riddles, photos, and more.

StarChild: A Learning Center for Young Astronomers

http://starchild.gsfc.nasa.gov/docs/StarChild/shadow/StarChild.html

A good introductory Web site for the youngest stargazers, with information presented for children at different levels.

Exploration in Education

http://marvel.stsci.edu/exined-html/exined-home.html

A fantastic site sponsored by the Space Telescope Science Institute, with downloadable storybooks on space exploration, art by kids, asteroid impacts, and much more.

NASA's Quest Project

http://quest.arc.nasa.gov

A fun, interactive site filled with special "classroom" projects on selected topics, including live broadcasts from space and virtual conferences on exciting space missions.

Spacecraft Galileo at Jupiter

http://eis.jpl.nasa.gov/~skientz/galileo

Learn all about the *Galileo* mission to Jupiter and its moons at this easy-to-use site. Lots of pictures, Q & A, and more.

Cassini Spacecraft Kids Corner

http://www.jpl.nasa.gov/cassini/Kids

Fun, kid-oriented site exploring the *Cassini* mission to Saturn and its moon Titan.

Imagine the Universe

http://imagine.gsfc.nasa.gov/docs/homepage.html

A site designed by the High-Energy Astrophysics Learning Center to bring the universe alive for young browsers.

• SPACE BOOKS •

Space Explained: A Beginner's Guide to the Universe

(Robin Scagell, 1996)

An easy-to-read explanation of the universe and the forces of nature. Illustrated with detailed photos and drawings that make space come alive.

Do Your Ears Pop in Space?

(R. Mike Mullane, 1997)

Five hundred fun, informative, and intriguing questions about space travel, with answers provided by a real shuttle astronaut.

The Cartoon Guide to Physics

(Larry Gonick and Art Huffman, 1990)

An easy-to-read, funny cartoon guide to the laws of physics and the forces of the universe.

The Universe Explained

(Colin A. Ronan, 1994)

A fun, information-packed guide to the wonders and mechanics of the universe. Filled with photos, illustrations, and diagrams.

Amazing Space: A Book of Answers For Kids
(Ann-Jeanette Campbell, 1997)
Easy-to-read questions and answers on everything from the stars and planets to astronomy and space travel. Includes glow-in-the-dark star stickers.

The Handy Space Answer Book
(Phillis Engelbert and Diane L. Dupuis, 1998)
This impressive volume answers 1,200 of the most common questions about the universe, our solar system, and the history and future of space exploration in clear language.

Space Exploration
(Carole Stott, 1997)
Part of the "EyeWitness Books" series, this photo-packed volume is a treat for the eyes and an easy introduction to everything from the origin of the universe to what lies ahead in space science.

Murmurs of Earth: The Voyager Interstellar Record
(Carl Sagan, 1978)
Learn all about the first detailed message humankind has ever sent to the stars.

The Space Shuttle Operator's Manual
(Kerry Mark Joels and Gregory P. Kennedy, 1988)
An in-depth guide for anyone who's ever wondered what it's like to fly on the shuttle. Includes diagrams of the interior, countdown and checklist procedures, space food menus, and more.

Look Inside Cross Sections: Space
(Moira Butterfield, 1994; Nick Lipscombe and Gary Biggin, illus.)
Amazing cutaway diagrams peer into the workings of twelve different spacecraft, tracing technology from the *Mercury* capsule to the Hubble Space Telescope.

Mysteries of the Universe
(Nigel Hawkes, 1995)
A beautifully illustrated exploration of myths, legends, and unsolved mysteries of the universe. Perfect for young readers.

The Friendly Guide to the Universe
(Nancy Hathaway, 1994)
An in-depth guide to the history of astronomy and what humankind has learned about the universe. Useful to space buffs or readers learning about the subject for the first time.

Alien Contact: The First Fifty Years
(Jenny Randles, 1997)
The world's leading UFOlogist details every significant sighting since 1947, when pilot Kenneth Arnold's report of a UFO created the phrase "flying saucer."

• SPACE FILMS AND VIDEOS •

FICTION

Star Trek: The Motion Picture
(William Shatner, Leonard Nimoy, DeForest Kelley, 1979)
The crew of the *Enterprise* is reunited to save Earth from a mysterious space probe. This film offers an amusing look at one possible future of humankind's first probes sent into space.

The Right Stuff
(Sam Shepard, Ed Harris, Dennis Quaid, 1983)
Extremely realistic re-creations of spaceflight highlight this epic film on the birth of the Space Race and America's first seven astronauts.

Contact
(Jodie Foster, Matthew McConaughey, James Woods, 1997)
Based on astronomer Carl Sagan's best-selling book of the same name, *Contact* tells the story of a SETI astronomer who makes contact with an alien civilization. Features very impressive images of the entire universe.

E.T. the Extra-terrestrial
(Henry Thomas, Drew Barrymore, 1982)
Classic fantasy about a young boy's friendship with a frightened extraterrestrial accidentally stranded on Earth and the adventures involved in finding a way back home.

Close Encounters of the Third Kind
(Richard Dreyfuss, Teri Garr, Melinda Dillon, 1977)
Classic tale of humankind's first official contact with friendly extraterrestrials, as seen through the eyes of an ordinary person mysteriously drawn to the encounter.

Stowaway to the Moon
(Lloyd Bridges, John Carradine, 1975)
An eleven-year-old boy dreams of becoming an astronaut and accidentally gets sent into

space on a lunar mission. When trouble befalls the spacecraft, the stowaway gets a chance to save the day.

The First Men in the Moon
(Edward Judd, Lionel Jeffries, 1964)
Dramatic special effects highlight this adaptation of science fiction author H.G. Wells's classic tale of man's first voyage to the Moon.

NON-FICTION

Cosmos (13-episode series)
(Carl Sagan, 1980)
Famed astronomer Carl Sagan takes viewers on an epic journey from the beginning of creation to the future of space exploration. Travel to forty locations on Earth and hundreds in space.

Apollo 13
(Tom Hanks, Kevin Bacon, Bill Paxton, 1995)
The true story of the nearly disastrous *Apollo 13* mission, when an explosion in space forced cancellation of a Moon landing and three brave astronauts struggled to return home alive.

Stephen Hawking's Universe
This three-volume video series (narrated by astrophysicist Stephen Hawking) takes viewers on a journey to the distant past and future, exploring countless mysteries of the universe.

For All Mankind
(1989)
The story of NASA's *Apollo* flights to the Moon and the astronauts involved, assembled from hundreds of hours of archival footage.

• SPACE CD-ROMS •

3-D Tour of the Solar System
(Paul Schenk, David Gwynn, and James Tutor)
Spectacular 3-D images of the Sun, the planets, and their moons, taken in stereo by astronauts and NASA space probes. Comes complete with 3-D viewing glasses.
(Windows, Mac, Unix)

Hubble Library of Electronic Picturebooks
(Space Telescope Science Institute)
This CD features sixteen books' worth of space images and artwork, including many images from the Hubble Space Telescope. *(Windows, Mac)*

RedShift 2
(Maris)
An award-winning journey through the entire universe, featuring hundreds of thousands of stars and dozens of animations and movies. Ideal for beginners and experts alike. *(Windows, Mac)*

A Brief History of Time
(Stephen Hawking)
A CD-ROM version of Hawking's popular book on space, time, black holes, and the ultimate fate of the universe. Narrated by Stephen Hawking. *(Windows, Mac)*

PCs in Space
A fun, interactive educational program about computers and space, designed for enthusiasts ages eight to eighteen. Features thousands of color images and movies. This software is available on CD-ROM and can be downloaded for free from the Internet. *(Mac, Windows)*
For web download, visit: http://www.jnt.com

The Voyager Interstellar Record
(the Planetary Society)
The *Voyager* Interstellar Record contains pictures of Earth, a description of humans and animals, greetings written in every known language, and a selection of sounds and music. *(Mac, Windows)*

Connie & Bonnie's Birthday Blastoff
(Active Arts, Inc.)
An interactive tour through the solar system with fun cartoon characters and built-in coloring book. Full of fun riddles about our universe and other activities to learn as you go. *(Windows, Mac)*

Venus Explorer
(Romtech)
Have the entire surface of Venus right at your fingertips! A fun, easy-to-use, fascinating way to explore Earth's sister planet in detail, using the same images mapped by NASA's *Magellan* spacecraft. *(Windows, Mac)*

Appendix

In the early years of the space program, an astronaut waited until he had landed safely and debriefed NASA officials before telling the world about his experiences in space. Today's astronauts can post their "daily space journals" on the Internet, sharing the wonders of space and their life in zero-g with the entire globe while their mission is still underway!

• AN ASTRONAUT'S JOURNAL •

Astronaut David Wolf was born in 1956, in Indianapolis, Indiana. He enjoys many sports, including aerobatic flying, scuba diving, waterskiing, and handball. In 1978, he graduated with a science degree in electrical engineering from Purdue University. Four years later, he earned a medical degree from Indiana University and went to work at the Medical Sciences Division of Johnson Space Center, a division of NASA.

Dr. Wolf is a celebrated inventor and microgravity (zero-g) specialist. He has developed new medical procedures to monitor astronauts in orbit. In 1990, David entered astronaut training and was cleared for spaceflight a year later. He has flown aboard two Space Shuttle missions, STS-58 (October 16–November 1, 1993) and STS-86 (September 25, 1997–October 5, 1997). Three days after the launch of STS-86, David left the shuttle to begin a four-month stay aboard the *Mir* space station, joining Russian cosmonauts Anatoly Solovyev and Pavel Vinogradov. He was picked up from *Mir* by Space Shuttle mission STS-89 and returned home on January 31, 1998.

The following are excerpts from David's letters home, describing his life in space. *(All excerpts reprinted courtesy of NASA.)* To read more of David Wolf's "Letters Home" from *Mir*, visit: http://shuttle-mir.nasa.gov/shuttle-mir/ops/crew/letters/wolf

DAVID WOLF (RIGHT) AND FELLOW ASTRONAUT ABOARD *MIR* ▲

October 6, 1997

"It's a bigger job than one might think when every item you touch just floats off if you don't Velcro it, or strap it down, or bungee it in place. Great—my long lost—and invaluable—electric shaver just floated by. The first place to look for lost items is in one of the air filters. A bowling ball would find its way there in 0 gravity."

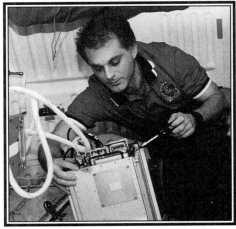

October 31, 1997

"Apparently it takes longer than three weeks to get totally used to no gravity. I still look up at the gas analyzer on the ceiling and wonder, for a moment, how I'll get up there to read it and find myself momentarily surprised to discover that I can just fly on up. I continue to try and put things "down," foolishly thinking it might stay put. Naturally, it quickly gets lost. I get my hands too full, and then am a bit slow to simply let go and then sort it out. I also forget to use the ceiling as a surface. . . . Don't worry though. I have plenty of time to figure it out."

November 14, 1997

"I've traveled roughly seventeen million miles since we left the crew quarters at Cape Kennedy, not including the van ride to the pad. But who's counting. In fact, Earth seems a bit dreamlike these days, as we are connected only by crackling voices on the radio and the photographs brought along and our memories."

December 22, 1997

"There are two things we never get used to in space. Looking at our Great Planet Earth and missing the great people on it. Since you can't be here and I can't be there, e-mail sure helps us share our experiences."

DAVID WOLF (BOTTOM ROW, LEFT) WITH FELLOW ASTRONAUTS ABOARD *MIR* ▲

Index

Aldrin, Edwin "Buzz" (astronaut), 57, 116
Alien astronauts, 49
Animals in space, 54–55
Antimatter, 44
Apollo 1 (space disaster), 61
Apollo 13 (near disaster), 62–63
Apollo 14 mission, 58
Armstrong, Neil (astronaut), 57, 116
Artificial intelligence, 80
Asteroids, 16, 17, 89. *See also* Meteors
Astrology, how different then astronomy, 11
Astronauts
  addresses to write-to famous ones, 115–116
  living in space, 98–100
  mission patches, designing, 97
  personal items allowed in space, 97
  training to become, 93–95
  using the bathroom in space, 99
Astronomer, becoming amateur, 117

Big Bang theory, 8, 10, 12, 15, 114
Big Crunch, 114
Biosphere 2 (research project), 111–112
Black Holes, 45–46
Books to read about space, 120–122
Calendar, used to explain the universe, 9–10
Cassini, Giovanni (scientist), 75, 76
Cassini (space probe), 75–77, 89
CD-Roms about space, 123–124

Chaffee, Roger B. (astronaut), 61
Challenger (space shuttle disaster), 64–65, 66
Comets, 16, 31–32
Copernicus, Nicolaus (scientist), 22
Cosmic Calendar, 9–10
Cosmos (book and television program), 10
Creationists, belief in God creating the Universe, 9

Deep Space 1 (DS1), spaceship, 80
Deep Space 4 (DS4), spaceship, 109
Definitions, 15–16
Dinosaurs, disappearance of, 90–91
Discovery (space shuttle), mission patch, 97
Drake, Frank (astronomer), 47
Earth (planet), 28–30
  atmosphere of, 29
Ecliptic plane, 26
Einstein, Albert (mathematician), 14
Endeavor (space shuttle), 66–67
Europa (Jupiter's moon), 73–74
Event horizon, 45–46
Extraterrestrial life, 47–48
  attempts to communicate with, 77, 78

Freedom (space station), 104
Galaxies, 15, 16
Galileo Galilei (scientist), 72
Galileo mission, 71–73, 120
Giotto (space probe), 32
Glenn, John (astronaut), 94

God, belief he created the universe, 9
Goddard, Robert H. (rocket pioneer), 51
Gravitons, 44
Great Attractor, 83
Grissom, Virgil "Gus" (astronaut), 61
Halley's comet, 31–32
Hawking, Stephen (physicist), 46, 124
Hot air balloons (space probes), 76–77
Hubble, Edwin (scientist), 14
Hubble Space Telescope, 19, 59, 84–85, 124
Huygens, Christiaan (physicist), 76
Huygens (space probe), 75, 89

Interplanetary Network (IPN), 100
Jet Propulsion Laboratory (JPL), 47–48, 70, 118
Jupiter, 32–33, 49
  Europa (moon), 73–74
  space probes to, 71–73, 77–78
Kepler, Johannes, 12–13
Kuiper Airborne Observatory (KAO), 85
Launch preparations, 96–97
Levy, David (astronomer), 73
Light pollution, 83
Light, speed of, 12
Light-year, 11–12
Lippershey, Hans (inventor), 72, 83
Lovell, James, (astronaut), 116

Magellan (spacecraft), 28
Mars (planet), 30–31

Mars (planet), *cont.*
  future plans to colonize, 112
  missions to, 69–71
Mars Global Surveyor (space
  probe), 70–71
Mars Pathfinder (space probe),
  69–70
McAuliffe, Christa
  (schoolteacher/astronaut),
  64–65, 66
Mercury (planet), 26–27
Meteorites, 16, 48
Meteors, 89–92
Milky Way, 16, 17, 21
Mir (space station), 103–104
Moon, 16, 39–41
  first landing on, 56–58
  missions to, 67
Moon trees (from seeds in space),
  58–59
Moons
  names of 38–39
Movies about space, 122–123

NASA (National Aeronautics and
  Space Administration) 44, 117
  astronaut selection program,
  93–95
  program for kids, 115
Neptune (planet), 35–36
Neutrinos (particles), 42, 43
Newton, Isaac (scientist), 13
Next Generation Space Telescope
  (NGST), 86
Oberth, Herman (rocket pioneer), 52
Oort, Jan Henrick (astronomer), 20
Outerspace, 11
Particles, 45
Pathfinder (mission to Mars), 69–70

Planetary rings, 25
Planetary Society, 10
Planets, 16, 23, 25, 26
  how they got named, 24
  new ones, 37–38
Pluto (planet), 23, 36–37, 109
  Charon (moon), 36–37, 85
Proxima Centauri, 18, 20

Robots, 110–111
Rockets, 51–52, 80
Russian space program, 52–53,
  56–57, 60, 102–103
Sagan, Carl (astronomer), 9, 10,
  49, 70
Saturn (planet), 33–34, 75
"Schoolteachers in Space"
  program, 64–65
SETI (Search for Extraterrestrial
  Intelligence), 48
Shepard, Alan B. (astronaut), 58
Shoemaker, Eugene (astronomer), 73
Shoemaker-Levy 9 (comet), 89
Skylab (space station), 102–103
Solar flares, 22
Solar system, 16, 21
Solar wind, 109–110
Soyuz (space disasters), 61, 62
Space, 11
  Calendars, 81–82
  disasters, 60–66
  first men to walk in, 53
  trash in, 99–100
Space Age, timeline, 50–68
Space Camp (for public), 116–117
Space colonies, 111–113
  contest for students to design, 112
Space Mirror (memorial), 66
Space Observatories, 86, 107–108

Space probes, 67–80
Space race, 52–53, 56–57
Space shuttles, 64–67, 101, 106, 115
Space Stations, 102–106
Sputnik, 52, 53, 54
Stars, 17–19
Stonehenge, 81–82
Sun (star), 18, 21, 79
  death of, 113–114
Sunquakes, 22
Supercluster, 15, 17

Telescopes, 83–89
Terrestrial Planet Finder (TPF),
  86–87
Time, mystery of, 44–45
Tsiolkovsky, Konstantin (rocket
  pioneer), 52
Tunguska fireball (meteor), 91
Ulysses (space probe), 79
Universal Laws, 12–14
Universe, 8–9, 12– 15, 42, 43, 114
Unmanned space flights, 67–80
Uranus (planet), 34–35
Venus (planet), 27–28, 124
Verne, Jules (science fiction writer),
  50, 51
Vesta (asteroid), 31
Videos about space, 122–123
"Vomit Comet" (equipment), 95
Voyager 1 and 2 (space probes), 78
Volcanoes, 33

Web sites, 118–120
Weightlessness, 94–96
White, Ed (astronaut), 53–54, 61
Wolf, David (astronaut), journal of,
  125–126
Wormholes, 46